MISSION TRIPPING
A Comprehensive Guide to Youth Ministry Missions

By Danny Kwon

To my in-laws Giu and Jea Sook Kim, overseas full-time missionaries serving the Lord in remote places, risking their lives, spreading the gospel "Sent" for the good work of the Kingdom. You birthed a wonderful daughter, my wife, and birthed many churches around the world for the good work of the Kingdom.

To my retired senior pastor, Rev. Yong Kol Yi, always reflecting a heart for missions as a "sender," supporting missionaries near and far, as well as diligently supporting the short-term mission efforts of our church and youth group. You gave and inspired many for the good work of the Kingdom.

To the teenagers of our youth group, past, present, and even future, who have ventured with me to places near and far, who have sacrificed their time and vacation breaks to serve, who have served with me and my wife. You are the light of God. "Don't let anyone look down on you because you are young." You have done so much good for the good work of the Kingdom.

To my three children, now all older and the last of you soon off to college. Instead of traditional vacations, you were all willing to go on short-term mission trips each summer, and a few of them as a family. Mom and I love you so much. You have given so much for the good work of the Kingdom (and will continue to do so, I know).

To my wife of now 20 years. You are an inspiration to many. A professor and counselor who is so busy. But you let me take many of my 44 short-term mission trips while you stayed home and supported the efforts of our mission trips in that way. The spouse who lets their partner go away for the mission trip should also be commended for his/her good service toward the mission trip. You have done the most and greatest for the good work of the Kingdom.

Mission Tripping
Copyright © 2017 by Danny Kwon

Publisher: Mark Oestreicher
Managing Editor: Tamara Rice
Cover Design: Adam McLane
Layout: Marilee R. Pankratz
Creative Director: St. Patrick

All rights reserved. No part of this book may be reproduced in any form by any electronic or mechanical means including photocopying, recording, or information storage and retrieval without permission in writing from the author.

All Scripture quotations, unless otherwise indicated, are taken from the Holy Bible, New International Version®, NIV®. Copyright ©1973, 1978, 1984, 2011 by Biblica, Inc.™ Used by permission of Zondervan. All rights reserved worldwide. www.zondervan.com The "NIV" and "New International Version" are trademarks registered in the United States Patent and Trademark Office by Biblica, Inc.™

Scripture quotations marked ESV are from the ESV® Bible (The Holy Bible, English Standard Version®), copyright © 2001 by Crossway, a publishing ministry of Good News Publishers. Used by permission. All rights reserved.

ISBN-10: 1-942145-27-6
ISBN-13: 978-1-942145-27-1

The Youth Cartel, LLC
www.theyouthcartel.com
Email: info@theyouthcartel.com
Born in San Diego
Printed in the U.S.A.

CONTENTS

FOREWORD

My wife, Gina, and I are standing on a street corner in the largest city in the world. But this isn't just any street corner in Tokyo. This is Shibuya Crossing, better known as the planet's busiest intersection. Each time the lights turn, 2,500 pedestrians cross from one side of the street to the other.

Shibuya Crossing doesn't look like your average intersection in the United States. It doesn't have four corners and a cute little timer showing us how many seconds until we cross the street towards our destination. No, Shibuya Crossing has so many lanes of traffic converging from different angles that it looks like a plate of spaghetti noodles from above. And the crossing options. So many crossing options. Who knew that you could simply take the diagonal and walk kitty corner on a painted crosswalk! And yet, you better know where you want to be at Shibuya Crossing, because the moment the vehicle traffic stops, 2,500 people will be making sure they get as quickly as possible to their desired side of the street and nothing will be allowed to stop them, including the bewildered American travelers that are unintentionally causing a logjam. Gina and I are to either jump into the stream and go with the flow or try to stop and be crushed by the locals trying to get on with their day. So, we choose to jump into the stream and ride the physical current of humanity at the world's busiest intersection.

Shibuya Crossing is a microcosm of every country in the world. It may look confusing, disorienting, and even overwhelming to someone who has never been there before. And yet, the people of Tokyo have made Shibuya Crossing what it is today because an intersection like this suits their culture's needs. It may not be how I would create this intersection. It may not be how you would create this intersection. But it's exactly how the Japanese would create this intersection!

MISSION TRIPPING

My wife and I have traveled to all corners of the world, including the six major continents. One thing that we find in each and every country we visit is that the people have developed a rhythm of life that makes use of their culture and environment. The people of Japan are very accustomed to crowded spaces, so 2,500 people crossing the street at once is just a normal occurrence. This is also the same for you, the reader. The place you live has developed, grown, and been shaped by your culture and environment. I grew up in Duluth, Minnesota. Our downtown has enclosed "skywalks" that cross over our streets, so that people don't have to go outside in the frozen winter. Crosswalks over the streets to keep us warm! Who knew? If you pause to think about what makes your home unique, you'll see the fingerprints of your local culture and environment all over the place.

This is what makes short-term missions such a powerful experience. We get to leave our own home, culture, and environment, and drop into an entirely different home, culture, and environment—basically overnight. When we first started Praying Pelican Missions, it was mind-blowing to me that I could wake up in my bed at home in Minnesota and have lunch the same day in a Central American jungle with new friends! The world got very small, very quickly. And yet as the number of our international friends and ministry partners grew, God kept calling me back to the same place and perspective as I was entering into all these different countries. *I am visiting someone else's home. Their way of life is based on culture and environment, just like mine is. I need to listen, observe, and learn their culture and pace of life. There is a reason why they do things differently than me.*

I remember one of my first visits to Belize. A few of us Americans were eating dinner at the home of a new friend, and they served us pig tail as part of the meal. That's right, pig tail. Picture a jumbo hot dog, shaved, and then cut into six-inch pieces and boiled. That's pig tail. My first thought was "I can't eat this. I've never eaten anything like this. I don't even know *how* to eat this!"

After those initial thoughts and a moment of feeling my own palms sweat, I looked up to see how the others in our group were doing with the meal. The Belizean family we were eating with was so pleased to have visitors who wanted to share in their culture with them. So, we watched how the Belizeans ate their pig tail. It turned out the pig tail was a meaty compliment to the rice, potatoes, and other starchy foods on our plates. The Belizean family would cut some meat (kind of like ham) off the pig tail and combine it with their plain white rice. It added some protein to a meal that lacked protein in a culture that couldn't afford all the prime cuts of meat we've come to expect in our American homes. So, I ate the pig tail. Candidly, it wasn't my favorite meal, based on flavor, because I wasn't used to pig tail at my dinner table. But it was one of my most memorable meals, because I'm now sharing it 15 years later in a book on short-term missions!

The beauty of short-term missions is the opportunity to see and learn from a culture that is different from ours, literally overnight. When we visit another culture and our hearts are in a place that is prepared to learn from the new culture, short-term missions is such a beautiful experience. But here's the non-negotiable when it comes to missions: Our hearts must be at a place that seeks to listen and learn *first*. We must observe and learn from the culture, just like Gina and I needed to do at Shibuya Crossing in Tokyo. If we enter into a new culture with hearts that are prideful, then we'll find ourselves wanting to criticize the local culture and wanting to teach and show them the "right" way to live. This spirit is disastrous in any situation, and it has led to harming many people's perception of not just missions but the Christian church as a whole. Knowing that *we don't have all the answers, we make plenty of mistakes,* and *we're on this mission trip to learn and to love like Jesus* is the best place to start. And the funny thing is, it doesn't take any special degree, education, or qualifications to be ready to serve in Christian missions. It simply takes a humble heart to love the world just as Jesus loves us.

"For even the Son of Man did not come to be served, but to serve, and to give his life a ransom for many." – Mark 10:45

I pray that as you prepare for your short-term missions experience, you see God's beauty in the cultural differences. That the differences are opportunities to grow and love in a brand new way, and that you can bring that fresh perspective to another important mission field that needs people to serve and love like Jesus: your very own home town!

God bless you on your upcoming mission trip.

In Christ,

Matt Pfingsten
President, Praying Pelican Missions
February, 2004
Tokyo, Japan

INTRODUCTION

Two million. There are *two million* 13- to 17-year-olds who go on religious mission team project trips every year.

I read this statistic a few years back, and it still boggles my mind and seems unbelievable. However, while it was a staggering assessment, it seemed legitimate coming from a respected seminary professor, and it was based on data from one of the most noted sociologists studying the religious practices of teenagers and young adults. This is what Professor Robert Priest said exactly: "The sociologist Christian Smith, based on national random survey data, reports that 29 percent of all 13- to 17-year-olds in the US have 'gone on a religious missions team or religious service project,' with 10% having gone on such trips three or more times. That is, his data indicates that far more than two million 13- to 17-year-olds go on such trips every year."[1] This number still blows my mind!

After reading a wide and vast array of sources for this book on short-term mission (STM) trips, as well as an exhaustive amount of material related to STM trips for and with youth groups, I can tell you that there are a variety of efforts to pinpoint how many people, including teenagers and youth groups, participate in STM trips each year. Yet, there are discrepancies in the statistics and not much consensus. What is very clear, however, is that STM trips for youth groups do have an important function, despite the negative feedback and pushback about STM trips in recent years, which I will highlight later in this book. Moreover, STM trips for youth groups are as popular as ever for churches, and there are many reasons for this.

Author and researcher Terry Linhart notes that "for numerous youth ministry leaders, short-term cross-cultural service trips offer a brief moment for students to experience faith with a new passion and purpose that counters a consumeristic culture's influence."[2] Adventures in Missions Director Seth Barnes also has stated that many youth leaders agree their summer mission trip projects have greater impact than any other single event they schedule.[3] And finally, author and international ministry advocate Paul Borthwick has said that when it comes to mission trips, discipleship is the key to well-prepared youth. If there is discipleship, the impact of an STM trip will produce fruit long after it ends.[4]

Personally, I am a pastor of youth and families—at my current church for over 22 years—and I'm an STM trip junkie. I love these trips. I have been on 44 short-term mission trips, 19 of them outside of the US, in other words international/overseas STM trips. There are many reasons why I love these trips, but as you can probably guess, the biggest reason is because I believe in them. I have seen the potential and the spiritual impact they have for the life transformation of teenagers and the impact on their faith journeys long after youth group. I also know that in recent years, there has been much critique of the value of STM trips in general, as well as the value of STM trips specifically for youth groups.

I have read the critiques and I can appreciate where they are coming from. In fact, this book will discuss many of them. But my general counter to these critiques is that many of them may be true, *if* you are *not* doing short-term missions right. If you don't have the correct expectations and rationale (and theology) for these STM trips, if you don't prepare and train your teens and adult leaders, if you don't work intimately with your church leadership, if you don't carefully consider factors such as cost, if you don't work with the indigenous, local people on the field, and if you don't have a realistic picture of your "return on investment" (ROI), then yes, one can find many areas of critique for these trips. However, if done well, while there will always be places for critique and improvement, STM trips can have a lasting impact for youth groups, churches, and in the lives of the participants, both the "senders" and "goers." Ultimately, they can have an important and lasting impact on those we are going to minister to and with.

With those truths in mind, this is a resource and guide for taking youth groups and teenagers on STM trips and doing these trips well. I've written it for church leaders, youth pastors, youth workers, and volunteers as well. Think of it as a general handbook, which is both informational (containing theology and rationale for missions with youth) and very practical. This book will offer practical tips, ideas, and advice I have picked up from my 44 mission trips, as well as from others whose wisdom I've been gleaning along the way. It will be broken down into five sections:

> Section I: An Overview of Youth Ministry & Missions
> Section II: Going There: Preparing to Go
> Section III: Being There: On the Field
> Section IV: Back Again: Home Life
> Section V: 15 Meetings: Before, During, & After Your Trip

Mission Tripping is intended to be read and used before you go on an STM trip—perhaps long before you even *consider* going on one. As you will read in Section V, there is also a companion to this book called *Mission Tripping: An Interactive Journal*, which is the teen STM trip preparation guide created to be paired with this book. It contains—besides many prayer and journaling prompts—a workbook for 15 meetings that will help you prepare your teens for an STM trip. Section V of this book holds not only the contents of the Interactive Journal but also special insights for you as you lead those meetings and walk your group through it.

Finally, another important reason I wrote this book for churches and youth ministries is because of a short-term youth mission trip that I was not actually physically present for as a youth pastor. In 1995, we had a terrible tragedy on an STM trip led by a colleague. One of our teens drown in a river while swimming on a very hot day in rural Mexico. It was long before cell phones. Even recently when I traveled there, it was still hard to get cell phone reception in that area. Back then, this location only had dirt roads, no running water, and extreme poverty. When it rained, you would be walking in mud up to your calves because there was no pavement. In fact, we only showered when it rained because of the lack of water. For meals, the generous but impoverished people in that area would have to kill a chicken that had been frolicking on their front yard that morning. (It was fascinating but grotesque one year when I saw one of the local people slaughter a cow for our team and the village, so we could celebrate our team's service to the community as our trip was ending.)

It was in this desolate, rural, and poor village that our teen died in the river. I had been to this mission trip location prior to 1995, but I couldn't make it that year. No family, no church, no youth ministry, no youth pastor, should ever have to deal with the death of a teen. I have had this terrible experience of death in our youth group a few times—some due to accidents and others due to terminal illness. It is horrifying every time. The saying that "no parent should have to bury their child" cuts to the heart of the horrendous emotions one experiences, even if the death is not directly one's child. But in the case of a terrible accident, where death is unexpected and perhaps could have been prevented, the pain seems to cut even deeper. It still does today.

In the midst of this tragedy and loss in 1995, something miraculous happened. The morning before his death, the teen led a team devotional based on John 12:24 that says, "Very truly I tell you, unless a kernel of wheat falls to the ground and dies, it remains only a single seed. But if it dies, it produces many seeds."

No one, of course, knew he was going to die that day, and in the weeks after his death, this boy's parents, who were supposed to send him off to college a few weeks after the trip, decided to take all the tuition they had saved for 18 years of his life and build a church in the small village where he died. I still think back with disbelief. The response of the parents could have been suing the church or getting angry at the team leaders, but by God's grace, it wasn't.

Today, that "kernel of wheat" has now led to not only one church being built, but 12 new churches being planted from that location. There are now paved roads into that small village town, a school for children to attend, and a water collection system that enables our team to shower when we go there. I understand this is an extraordinary and miraculous story. However, what I do believe from this experience is that any STM trip—be it imperfect, or in this case tragic—can produce many seeds. Churches and youth ministries just need to learn to do these trips well and to "die" to themselves so that many seeds can be produced. We need STM trips. And most of all, we need them because as Jesus said, "The harvest is plentiful, but the workers are few." Youth groups and teenagers can be those workers for the harvest. So, let's go!!!

SECTION I
AN OVERVIEW OF YOUTH MINISTRY & MISSIONS

CHAPTER 1 | THREE IDEAS: MISSIONS, SHORT-TERM MISSIONS, AND YOUTH MINISTRY

Research has shown that until 2005, local churches have been the most common place for teenagers to be involved in service activities and teenagers have learned about volunteer activities through the church more than any other organization.[5] Moreover, the church has always been a place where teenagers could be involved in meaningful service to the community and world and use these experiences to learn and grow in their faith. However, the focus of this book is STM trips with teenagers in the context of youth groups and youth ministry. It's very specific.

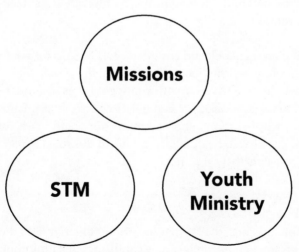

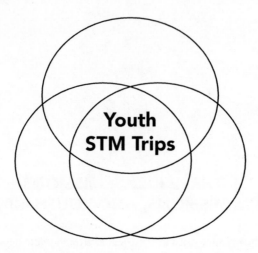

It's not just about missions. It's not just about mission trips that are short term. It's not just about teenagers and youth ministry and missions. This book is specifically focused on STM trips with teenagers in youth group and church settings. In other words, I am focusing on the STM mission trips that churches take, most often (but not exclusively) in the summer time, with youth group teens who are off from school.

So, in working on this book and considering STM trips for youth groups, much of my writing focused on helpful tips, guidelines, and insights to help make STM trips with youth groups as meaningful as possible. However, it was clear that the three distinct elements directing my focus (missions, short-term missions, and STMs for youth groups) needed to be discussed briefly in this first chapter as the distinct concepts that they are.

MISSIONS

In considering missions, the "s" that sometimes differentiates the two words *mission* and *missions* can be confusing. In a multitude of precedent literature related to the topic of mission versus missions, the distinction of missions with an "s" is that it refers to the work of the church in reaching people for Christ. Mission—no "s"—often has a broader definition that includes not only the former but also deeper implications about our identity and place in this world and the nature of God himself. This book will focus on the more concrete and literal teaching of mission/missions as we probably all understand it— reaching people for Christ—and I'll be using it with and without an "s."

Eckhard Schnabel, a leading New Testament scholar who has studied the idea of mission (or missions) in the New Testament, says the following: "The argument that the word *mission* does not occur in the New Testament is incorrect. The Latin verb *mittere* corresponds to the Greek verb *apostellein*, which occurs 136 times in the New Testament (97 times in the Gospels, used both for Jesus having been 'sent' by God and for the 12 being 'sent' by Jesus)."[6] He offers a clear foundation for missions in Scripture. It is a biblical teaching and priority. The apostles themselves, by definition of who they were, were those being "sent out." Similarly the book of Acts demonstrates the "sending" of the church as we see even more go out as missionaries. In considering a theology of missions and our teenagers, there are many ways we can expound upon it—a biblically driven theology here could be vast. However, I personally have three foundational understandings of missions that I teach to my youth group.

First, missions is one of the primary callings of the *church*. Theologian Edmund Clowney, in his book *The Church*, discusses many elements of what the church is biblically.[7] But one of the more profound yet simple truths of why missions exists is the fundamental meaning of *church* in the New Testament and the role of the church, which is to "gather." In fact, in the original Greek language, the word *church* actually holds the idea of "gathering."

This "gathering" function of the church has many nuances however. For example, it means to gather as a Body of Christ and to gather as his people. However, it was ultimately the mission of *God*, in Jesus Christ, to gather his people, as the great and original Missionary. Jesus came to gather his church and has called his people to gather others. The disciples of Jesus, for example, were called to missions as they were sent out—called to *gather* the poor and needy.

MISSION TRIPPING

As Matthew 12:30 says, "Whoever is not with me is against me, and whoever does not gather with me scatters." Gathering is essential and of the greatest priority for God's church. The fundamental definition of church then is not an address, not a location, not a place where the youth group meets, not just a place of worship, and not just a place of spiritual nurture. It is a gathering of God's people, a subsequent call for all his people to be gatherers with Jesus and share Jesus with others, so that others would gather. This is the heart of the church and subsequently missions. As Clowney discusses further, the identity of gathering is fundamental to understanding the mission of the church. It is the aspect of gathering that starts from the work of Jesus gathering his people, to the mission of the church, to continuing to gather others. This is vital as we teach "going out" to our youth group teens through STM trips. The church is not only the meeting place of the youth group and the starting point of their mission trip but, by definition, the church's mission (and youth group's mission) is to be gathered together by Christ and then gather others for Christ.

Second, another foundation to my understanding of missions is Matthew 28:16-20. The Great Commission. It is probably the most quoted passage of the Bible when it comes to missions. However, it is worth discussing in an effort to understand missions more deeply. It reads: "Now the eleven disciples went to Galilee, to the mountain to which Jesus had directed them. And when they saw him they worshiped him, but some doubted. And Jesus came and said to them, 'All authority in heaven and on earth has been given to me. Go therefore and make disciples of all nations, baptizing them in the name of the Father and of the Son and of the Holy Spirit, teaching them to observe all that I have commanded you. And behold, I am with you always, to the end of the age.' "

In this passage, what we can see is that Jesus does give a directive and specific commission to his disciples when he says "go." When I think of this idea of *commission*, it reminds me of the classic '80s movie *Top Gun*. Near the latter part of the movie, Tom Cruise (or "Maverick"), finishes Top Gun school for jet fighter pilots, and immediately after graduation, he and a few of his squadron are told they need to leave on a dangerous mission. This always reminds me of what a mission and commission are. The assignment is their mission. It is their commission. As Christians, we too are commissioned by God to go out on mission for him.

The disciples–*disciple* meaning "follower of Christ"—were not "super" Christians. They were tax collectors and fishermen. Ordinary, common people. In fact, right before Jesus commissioned them for his mission work, Matthew 28:17 says, "And when they saw him they worshiped him, but some doubted." In other words, these disciples were not perfect. They were filled with doubt and uncertainty, right before being sent out to go. This should give us hope as we consider the work of what mission is all about. It was a commission given to ordinary people.

On another note, theologian and seminar professor Phillip Bethencourt states in reference to this passage that Jesus is deploying the Kingdom and that he is sending his followers out as ambassadors of the Kingdom. He further states that "in the great commission, King Jesus issues his discipleship battle plan to the church because he possesses 'all authority in heaven and on earth' (Matthew 28:18). Jesus sends his soldiers to the front lines to engage the kingdom of darkness."[8] It is this church of his "soldiers" that is commissioned and deployed for his mission work. Hence, it is important to understand that although his commission is given to ordinary people, it is given with the *authority* of Jesus. More specifically, the commission is given to *Go* and *Make Disciples*. This is the imperative and is the thrust of what we must understand about missions. Missions is a commission for ordinary people—ordinary people who are commissioned with the authority and power of Jesus. I believe this is a vital aspect to convey to our teenagers as they prepare and go on their STM trips.

Thirdly and finally, Acts 1:8 is extremely helpful in understanding missions and the scope of it. It says, "But you will receive power when the Holy Spirit has come upon you, and you will be my witnesses in Jerusalem and in all Judea and Samaria, and to the end of the earth." Why this verse is so important is that in considering missions, we see missions is definitely a calling to "go" and go to the "ends of the earth." This verse specifically seems to connote the idea of the *travel* and *distance* aspect of missions. People often refer to the Apostle Paul's missions work as his missionary "journeys." Certainly, missions must be considered in terms of the journey that believers must make and the time and effort it takes to make these trips. However, in considering this verse, we can see that there are several locations mentioned for a reason.

There was a call to go to Jerusalem, which shows missions can be more local. There was a call to go to Judea and Samaria, which required more travel, perhaps about a day or so. Finally, there was call to go to the "ends of the earth," which you can imagine could be a much longer mission trip.

However, not only is the variety of distances/times something noteworthy from this verse, but for New Testament believers in the early church, it was probably shocking to see the Samaritans mentioned in these calls to missions. Samaritans were outcasts from the Jewish culture, yet there was a calling to go to the Samaritans as a mission field, as well as their local Jerusalem community. Hence, God called his people to even the most "rejected" or simply overlooked in the culture and times.

Overall, when considering Acts 1:8, youth can be challenged to see the amazing opportunity they have in "journeying" on an STM trip, but also that there are different types of journeys as well. Moreover, missions is not only about the variety of distances and times, but also about reaching the local community and those who are the rejected and outcast.

This understanding of missions will benefit our youth as we nurture in them a theology of missions that is not just "an event" they do in the summer. There are a variety of distances in our calling and a variety of people God has called Christians to go and be witnesses to. Missions is the calling of the church and the teens' lives both short term and long after the trip, for a variety of communities and people.

SHORT-TERM MISSIONS

In almost all the literature on STMs that I have read for this book—and that has been quite a lot—it is always described as a recent phenomenon of the church. The changing nature of the church and our perspective on missions is most often discussed as the major reason why STM trips have become such a phenomenon. Founder of Global Partnership Ministries Scott Kirby defines STM trips as missions for non-vocational missionaries, cross-cultural in nature, having specific tasks over predetermined or limited periods of time, with definite spiritual objectives.[9] According to missionary Daniel McDonough and STEM International founder Roger Peterson, STM trips can be defined as "the God-designed, repetitive deployment of swift, temporary non-professional missionaries."[10]

Additionally, Trinity Evangelical Divinity School's Robert Priest notes that the "duration of time" aspect of STM trips has changed over the years and that two weeks or less is what research indicates as the time period for most STM trips.[11] He goes on to define it as "limited, organized, cross-cultural mission efforts… without participants making a residency-based commitment of more than two years."[12] (Alternately, Terry Linhart of Bethel College defines the length of these trips as one to four weeks.)[13] What we can see from these definitions is that STM trips are typically unique in terms of time rather than the mission itself.[14]

The actual term "short-term missions" doesn't appear in the Bible. Many terms the church uses now do not necessarily appear in the Bible. However, short-term missions seems to have grown from a biblical foundation, contextualized to our modern day.

For example, one could argue, Jonah in the Old Testament was called to an STM that was a cross-cultural experience for him. In Luke 9 and 10, the disciples were sent out by Jesus and returned to him to report about their ministry. As discussed earlier, in Acts 1:8, the promise of the Holy Spirit and the call for the church in the New Testament to be witnesses of Christ calls them to go to Jerusalem, Judea, Samaria, and to the ends of the earth. In my trip to Israel, what I realized was that for those Jesus was speaking to, a "trip" to Jerusalem—versus Judea or Samaria or "the ends of the earth"—would take a shorter length of time. Of course, the "ends of the earth" is not a specific location, but even at face value, as previously discussed, it would be a much longer journey than being sent out to be witnesses for Jesus more locally. Again, it is evident that being sent out for Jesus involved different distances and lengths of travel.

In Acts 11:22, Barnabas is sent to Antioch from Jerusalem, which is an example of a "shorter" trip where a believer is sent out. Acts 8 is also a good example of a shorter mission trip, where Phillip is called to minister to the Ethiopian Eunuch. And frankly Acts, in general, is filled with the adventures of Paul making shorter ministry trips to visit and plant churches, to exhort and edify local believers, and to help churches in need.

In terms of youth groups and youth ministry, the idea of STMs make sense on so many levels. For example, if nothing else, no parent of a teenager is going to let his or her child go on a mission trip lasting a few years. You can see the unlikelihood of that ever happening. Teenagers typically have to finish high school, apply to college, and think about their futures. Long-term, career missions and missionary work may be a future calling, but for teenagers, it just can't happen.

In all this, I like what Scott Kirby notes in *Equipped for Adventure*.[15] He says that the contemporary STMs movement is a biblical and healthy expression of the American church's awakening of its missionary responsibility and a realization that evangelization no longer needs to be the work of the career missionary. Moreover, he notes that it can be the team effort of the vocational missionary, indigenous or local believers, the sending churches, and the short-term missionary.

YOUTH MINISTRY
(AND THE GENESIS OF STM TRIPS FOR YOUTH GROUPS)
In the context of contemporary youth ministry, many have seen STM trips become a *foundational* aspect of youth ministry, whereas camps,

events like concerts, and exciting weekly programs typically formed the foundation of youth ministry in the past.

Maybe that's partly due to globalization. Many practitioners and scholars have noted that teenagers being more connected to the world has been a driving force for youth STM trips. Author and theologian Andrew Root notes that STM trips in youth ministry have escalated with our cultural and societal transformations, particularly globalization.[16] He notes that we can travel the world now electronically—as we do with the internet, television, and cell phones—as well as physically. Hence, technology and travel have made things more accessible. Consequently, youth leaders can easily find a place to go for STMs, or a mission organization to go with, and can even connect with missionaries around the world. It's simply easier than it used to be.

But it's important to go back and understand the roots of youth ministry itself in the local church, as it has developed historically— as well as how a changing world has impacted practices in youth ministry, leading to activities/programs like STM trips. Much of the literature related to the history of youth ministry serves to illustrate how youth ministry got to where it is today, pointing, I believe, to how STM trips have become so important and popular in youth ministry. Furthermore, understanding the historical background of youth work helps one understand the ultimate impetus for youth pastors implementing STM trips in their middle school and high school ministries in the first place. One can see that there was an emergence of STM trips that were appropriate to a particular need in the history of youth ministry, which first began at the periphery of churches.

Historically, you could say that youth ministry has generally reacted to the needs of unchurched youth by creating effective communities that contextualized faith for the emerging generation. Other times, the church has been slow in creating paradigms to deal with the emergence of a new youth culture.

Educational ministries expert Mark Senter offers a comprehensive examination of the history of Protestant youth ministry in the United States.[17] His survey confirms that approaches to youth varied at different times and in different contexts in history. He categorizes four cycles of youth ministry, which include the first cycle of youth ministry from 1824-1875, where organizations and societies such as Young Men's Christian Association and various Sunday school associations were focused on ministry to young people. The second cycle of youth ministry was from 1881-1925, which emphasized the educational process in equipping and developing young people to experience God. Various denominational agencies were often behind these movements such as the Nazarene Young People's Society, Baptist Young People's Society, and the Epworth and Lutheran League. The third cycle of youth ministry was from 1933-1989, where youth ministry became relationally focused, especially in various parachurch movements. Lastly, Senter speaks of a fourth cycle of youth ministry, which began in the 1990s.

While Senter's chronological classifications of the cycles of youth ministry could be debated, his analysis serves the vital point that each cycle of youth ministry began with a ministry innovation to reach youth more effectively. Similarly, he notes that in the present cycle of youth ministry, it will require a far different response (or innovation) by youth ministry leaders and agencies, and he asks how faith communities can be restructured so that adolescents can become vital parts of the church long term again.

It is evident to me then why STM trips have become such an important part of youth ministry: They help meet this need. They are an outlet for helping connect teenagers to their churches long term. In fact, one helpful characteristic of these short-term mission trips for youth groups is "teenagers being challenged by the Great Commission of Jesus Christ to dedicate themselves to the fulfillment of Christ's mission on earth."[18]

Now, author and professor Jon Pahl's historical portrait of youth ministry in North America focuses on the development of four distinct youth ministry organizations from 1930 to 1999.[19] They include the Walther League (Lutheran), the Young Christian Workers

(YCW, Catholic), Youth for Christ (YFC, Evangelical), and the African-American congregational youth ministries. While there were differences in the youth ministry practices in each of these distinct groups, Pahl notes the commonality of problems and solutions that these youth ministries sought to resolve in their engagement with young people. Based on these commonalities within Pahl's historical analysis, one specific way this engagement can be accomplished is through teenagers' vertical integration into the church body through participation in the church. For example, inviting youth to participate in church leadership and activities. And STM trips can be a good way to get youth to *participate* in the church.

It's interesting to note that according to author and youth culture historian Jon Savage, America began to use the word "teenager" in the mid-1940s.[20] It coincided with America's victory in World War 2 and was a marketing term used by advertisers and manufacturers in regard to the spending power of adolescents. Consequently, as a target market, teenagers had become identified as a distinct group between 12 to 18 years of age with its own "rituals, rights, and demands."[21] Youth ministry author Chap Clark also notes that the middle of the twentieth century marked a new affirmed status for youth within American society.[22] Consequently, "teenagers had been granted a certified cultural niche that was enthusiastically embraced by adult culture."[23] Hence, following World War 2, and in conjunction with the advancement of the industrial age, a whole generation of youth became prominent figures with free time, extra money, and energy to burn.

This newfound status also began to impact organizations and institutions that nurtured and cared for youth, including the church. Senter asserts that this time period was the first major transition into a revolution for youth ministry, as well as when the actual term "youth culture" was introduced.[24] Ultimately, the creation of new methods and new spirituality in this generation proved to mark a new Christian movement that would impact ministry for generations to come. Similarly, parochial youth ministries rose up, and new missions structures such as Young Life and Youth for Christ exemplified youth ministry strategies that still have influence to the present day.

Most recently, in the last two decades, the church has met some of the needs of youth with the help of organizations such as Youth Specialties, Group, and others that function to equip and assist the local church.[25] These ministry organizations operate to serve youth groups specifically, which in many churches have become separate entities and specialized ministries, distinct from the main church body and not always functioning well, despite the abundance of resources now available.

Many recent studies have labeled present-day youth ministries as doctrinally thin, ethically tolerant, and consumer oriented, and show teens often leaving the church after high school.[26] Consequently, one could surmise that the increase in STMs has been a way to combat such problematic aspects of current youth ministry. STM trips with teenagers can be an excellent way to connect teenagers with the Great Commission and to move them into a deeper faith and discipleship. It enables them to connect with God's church, serve, and grow in faith, while still being an active part of the youth ministry.

As I personally examine the history of youth ministry, I believe it demonstrates that the church has come to different junctures before in ministry to teens and has been innovative and reinvented itself for the sake of the youth. Similarly, Wheaton's Howell describes STM trips in youth ministry as an innovation, and he also highlights that STMs have a positive personal and formative dimension for teens.[27]

CHAPTER 2 | NAVIGATING THE POTENTIAL PITFALLS

In outlining a brief theology of missions, the definition of STMs, and the rise of STMs in youth ministry in the previous chapter, I believe it's safe to say they are an important and positive development in ministry to our teenagers. However, not everyone feels this way. Over recent years especially, there has been much written about STM trips, and some related directly with youth STM trips. I am always sobered by such perspectives. For example, according to the book *Introducing World Missions*, "Critics have referred to short-term missions as the 'amateurization of missions' or 'drive-by missions.' "[1] Many critics also say that "long-term missionaries despise it."[2] However, there are those (like me) who believe in their value if they are done well and who are convinced that there are "best case scenarios" that make them effective and powerful for everyone involved. Yet, being for them or against them is a polarizing question, and it must be addressed.

I have a phrase I repeat in my church and especially with my youth group. It is sort of in the vein of the "God is good all the time; all the time God is good" thing. You can come to my youth group today and hear it. I always say, "Every church is good and every church is…" and the youth say "bad." In doing this, it is my hope to promote a healthy ecclesiology and view of church for teenagers. There is no perfect church. I understand that youth have good and bad perspectives of our church. Likewise, because I am part of a larger church, we get young people visiting all the time and wanting to switch churches and youth groups. And I tell every youth who visits under those circumstances that there is no perfect church and to remain in their youth group.

LEARNING FROM CRITICISM

In the same vein, I say there are good and bad mission trips. There is no perfect STM trip. I agree with Steve Corbett and Brian Fikkert, the authors of *When Helping Hurts,* who say in a related study guide, "As we consider how to engage in short-term mission trips well, we have to *assess our current efforts.*"[3] (Emphasis mine.) Moreover, they note that "a healthy, effective trip is more than one piece of our larger commitment to learning and engagement with what God is doing around the world and in our own communities." Paul Borthwick says, "The success of a service project, mission trip, or even a work day is often determined before the van leaves the church parking lot or the plane takes off."[4] Hence, it is worth hearing the critiques and assessing our STM trips (and those of others), learning from them, avoiding the potential pitfalls, and doing a better job preparing before we go on STM trips to make them successful. Here are seven of the most common critiques you'll hear about STM trips and my responses.

Critique 1: "STM trips are just glorified tourism." A few years ago, our youth group was on a mission trip in the Dominican Republic. Other churches and youth groups were also at this location and each day we would split off to different local areas and do different work. Our group was serving with a local pastor to refurbish his church, as well as do local outreach ministry and Vacation Bible School (VBS). About halfway through the trip, we had a leaders' meeting to discuss the last day of the trip, which was reserved for some rest and relaxation for the different teams. The host missionaries asked if we would like to visit a small market to get some souvenirs. Immediately, one of the leaders of the other group said that we should not, because it would make the mission trip like a vacation—like we were tourists instead of missionaries.

I vividly remember this leader's sentiments and understood his angle, although I still try to have at least one day of rest and fun on any mission trip I lead. But the reason I remember this trip and situation is because he and his youth group were the only team who brought nothing but shorts to wear on the trip. This may not seem like a major sin, but in the Dominican Republic, people only wear shorts in public places in their leisure time or if they are tourists. In other words, as the host missionary had stated, it was not culturally appropriate for our teams to be wearing shorts during the work day. Ultimately, this team leader did not take the time to learn about the proper dress and etiquette for the cultural context in which they would be serving. I wondered, with such lack of preparation, if he had taken this STM trip as seriously as he should have. How could someone be so fearful of even the briefest appearance of tourism completely overlook the equal if not greater importance of knowing the local customs? The fact was that he and his team already looked like tourists—the very thing he wanted to avoid—because of the oversight.

Either way, when a mission trip becomes or even appears to be a vacation or tourism, it no longer serves its purpose of being a mission trip. But I doubt any STM team would blatantly go on a tourism trip disguised as a mission trip. More likely, such situations arise unintentionally from a lack of preparation. For our youth, I try to outline the differences in our first preparation meeting every year. (I will highlight these differences in chapter eleven.)

Clear priorities and well thought out planning of a mission trip go a long way toward solving this problem. I like to start planning a mission trip at least 18 months in advance. For example, if I am planning a short-term mission trip for June of 2016, we begin to plan in January of 2015. That is the minimum: 18 months. It's not an exact science, but it begins our future STM trips on the right note. Moreover, even before that, we are praying and being sensitive to God's movement—watching for possible connections to missionaries, locations in which to serve, or mission organizations that may come across our radar.

As we pray and consider these things, we are also looking into the clear purpose and priorities for each trip. They might be different for each church. For our youth group, some of these values include…

1. Going to help and support the local missionary work already being done

2. Seeking to help nurture systemic change in the location we go to serve
3. Endeavoring to bring the gospel truth in word and deed
4. Promoting the spiritual growth and discipleship of each participant on our team as part of the STM process
5. Understanding our STM time is just part of the overall vision for missions and church for our youth group/church

Another aspect of our STM trips is that while each will have the foundation values I have noted, they will also have purposes specific to that particular location that are clearly outlined for our team's mission work and focus.

A youth worker friend recently went with his youth group to Maine to serve African refugees who have been displaced there. Another youth worker friend went to London, England, with his youth group to do street evangelism and share the gospel, particularly, with the large Muslim and Hindu communities there. In the summer of 2015, our youth group went to do outreach ministry to the marginalized Gypsy communities in Central Europe. At the same time, another team from my youth group traveled to rural Pennsylvania to repair homes. What you can see from the variety of trips I've mentioned is that there is a clear purpose and unique rationale for each of them. Hence, if you outline purpose and rationale clearly and regularly for your youth group and teams, it helps to keep the trip from becoming a tourist excursion.

I want to encourage you to plan early to help make your trips more purposeful. In fact, it also can be helpful to show your church, senior pastor, mission board, or outreach committee the clear intention of your STM trip. Even if you plan later (which I have done quite a few times), formulating clear values and purposes for each trip can move perception away from any hint that it is just tourism or some kind of pseudo-vacation. Moreover, in having clear values and purposes for each trip, we have a foundation from which to communicate the values and purposes to our teenagers and our parents. For me, I welcome being accountable to our church and our parents. We want the purposes of our trip to be clear and the core values of the STM trip to be evident, so it does not wind up turning into anything but ministry and service.

Ultimately, I understand this "tourism" critique of STM trips on many levels. When your STM trips don't have clear core values and don't have clear purposes, with goals in mind and ministry tasks outlined, they can devolve into tourism or other types of trips they weren't meant to be.

Critique 2: "STM participants can be prideful 'ugly Americans' in cross-cultural contexts—especially teenagers." Because I married a Canadian, I'm often called into accountability for being so US-centric in my views of the world and politics. The United States is a great country and I myself am both American and Korean. But I do frequently find myself thinking the US is the center of the world. For example, football as we know it the United States is not football in most parts of the world. However, it's easy to forget that.

In this vein, there has been much critique of STM trips and especially of teenager involvement. It has been noted that Americans often visit destinations both domestic and overseas and act rudely and insensitively (hence the term "ugly American"), not conforming to the norms and values of the local context. What is even uglier is when Americans come into cross-cultural contexts and think they know it all and have the best ways of doing things. Instead of being sensitive and learning from those who have lived in that context their whole lives, we act like superheroes, here to save the day for these "weak and feeble" people.

I can remember when we went to Haiti after the 2010 earthquake. The second year we went, we were asked to build and fortify the roofing on buildings and build a facility for a medical clinic. Knowing this, before we left I asked and received some donations to purchase power tools to be able to cut wood and sheet metal that would be used to fix and build roofs.

When we arrived on the first day of work to cut metal sheeting to fortify leaking roofs, I pulled out our power tools and began to show the Haitian locals, along with our team, how "things should be done," using the power tools. Perhaps because I have been working with teenagers so long, I was giving my team step-by-step instructions on how to measure the sheet metal, use the power tools, and find the leaking locations in the roofs to install them. After doing this for about 30 minutes, one of the Haitian gentlemen very politely said, "Can I say something?" I said, "Sure," and out of his back pocket he pulled a tool that seemed improvised but made for a job such as this. Then, he immediately showed me how to spot leaks in roofs from the inside of the buildings much better. Finally, he showed me an efficient system and human "assembly" line they use to get sheet metal up onto the roof and install it as well. Needless to say, I was pretty embarrassed. I had made a major mistake in doing mission work and probably offended my Haitian friends—all the while thinking because they had been so devastated by the earthquake, they needed *my* help. I was not only acting like an ugly American but also like the expert, when in reality they knew so much more than me.

Even domestically, unless trained and equipped for their STM trip, teenagers can act in ugly ways too. I say this with over 26 years of youth ministry experience and as someone who opens his house up to throngs of teenagers all the time. We understand that when you invite a group of teenagers over, they will bring different experiences from their own home lives. Some have been taught to be clean and tidy, while some teenagers have parents who probably clean up after them—or at least it seems that way, like they've never been taught to lift a finger in their homes. Our house can sometimes look like a disaster zone after a group of youth group teens has come over for chicken wings, Italian hoagies, and soda. Used napkins, cups with leftover soda, and buffalo wing bones can sometimes be found in different rooms of my house.

Please believe me when I say my wife and I love hosting teenagers. It has been a joy and privilege to do so, and we have intentionally bought a home 0.9 miles from church to be able to host our youth. However, when we take these young people on a mission trip, where we are often guests in other people's houses or stay at a host church for weeks at a time, it can get ugly. If youth haven't learned to be considerate or clean up after themselves in their own homes, then a mission trip can turn into the invasion of ugly and self-centered teenagers. Personally, I see this quite often on mission trips, both with my youth and when we partner with those of other youth groups.

Please understand this is not meant to be a critique of other youth ministries. I understand this self-centered behavior is part of the developmental nature and stage of life that teenagers are in. I know they are not always self-aware and are frequently focused on themselves. However, at times I cringe and wonder how those who are hosting a group of teenagers think and feel when the youth decide to turn on the television without asking or decide to lounge around for hours instead of working. When our mission teams do not practice leaving someone else's church or home "cleaner" than when we arrived, I feel horrible and wonder how the hosts feel about our youth group and mission team after. I remember one year, our group was working with another youth group and a paint fight erupted in the other group. I realize they were having fun, but quite a few of them got a lot of paint on themselves. When they decided to then lounge and lay out on the host family's lawn furniture and porch, I was aghast that we ruined quite a bit of both.

I have to acknowledge the potential validity of this critique of STM teams. Whether adults or teenagers, whether on foreign soil or in domestic communities, it is true that mission trips can be a place where the "ugly Americans" or "ugly teenagers" rear their heads. In coming to any STM trip location, the mindset that "we are the experts coming to help you" can really make Americans look "ugly."

One simple area where this shows up is when we are overseas and invited to a meal by a local family. Often, they are preparing the best of what they can offer because they do appreciate and value our work. However, the "best" of what they have to offer may be something completely different and strange to an American palate or what teenagers are used to.

I still shake my head with regret when I remember a trip to Mexico many years ago. We were served a stew by the hosts that they had been preparing all day. Admittedly, it did look strange, and I have personally never seen a stew or soup look so pitch black, even with my love for various mole sauces (and this wasn't a sauce but a soup).

However, when one of my teenagers, who assumed the hosts didn't speak English, said it looked "dangerous," one of the hosts looked up at us from across the room and said, "Why does it look dangerous? Would you like something else? We are sorry." I was heartbroken and crushed for this host family.

A STM trip can be an amazing opportunity to teach teenagers about what it means to *not* be an "ugly" American, what it means to be humble and respectful of host cultures and peoples. We can use these trips to help young people grow in self-awareness and "others-awareness." We can help youth be culturally sensitive and help them realize that we are not experts and heroes coming to serve at a location. The hosts and indigenous local people are our brothers and sisters in Christ and are equally part of the Body of Christ with us.

I love the book *Linking Arms, Linking Lives: How Urban-Suburban Partnerships Can Transform Communities,* which Ron Sider co-authored. I particularly like chapters five, six, and seven about "do and don'ts," particularly in helping those in urban and suburban contexts break down any stereotypes and avoid misunderstandings of each other in order to partner more effectively for ministry.[5] For example, it suggests that those in urban contexts should be open to seeing those in suburban contexts as people who have values and experiences that could help enrich their context. On the other hand, it suggests those from the suburban context need to be able to practice servanthood and not come in to urban contexts with a posture of teaching and leading. Overall, I have found that considering ideas like these ahead of time helps teenagers and adults be more sensitive to their actions and the perceptions of others.

Finally, as I consider this critique of the "ugly American/ugly teenager/expert," I am haunted by the many career missionaries who say that when STM teams come, it often sidetracks their ministries, ruins existing relationships with local people they have nurtured over the years, and causes years of rebuilding to restore these relationships. All because some STM teams come and do not realize the realities and impacts of their own behaviors.

My new senior pastor, who will begin ministry at our church this year, has been a career, long-term missionary for over 30 years. He says all the time, half-jokingly of course, that as mission teams have come and gone from the locations he has served as a missionary, he has secretly said to himself either "I hope they'll return again" or "I hope they never come back." This is so funny to me, but it is true of many career missionaries.

In our youth group, we have mottos that we talk about as we prepare and live out each day on the mission field. I'll outline them later in the book, and I hope they can serve to help your STM teams be *beautiful* teenagers and *humble* servants.

Critique 3: "STM trips are a waste of money." A huge critique of short-term mission trips is that they are a waste of money, that taking funds to go to a place to do ministry for a week or two is a waste of money. I understand this critique. Taking STM trips is a huge investment. However, what I can say is that as I look at the lives of teenagers these days, I see their schools have all kinds of trips—from ski club trips, to band trips to other states, club trips (which have students traveling to conferences), and graduation trips for twelfth graders where they spend a week in Disney World. Athletic camps in the summer are also extremely expensive, but some teens and parents shell out all kinds of money for them. Likewise, SAT/ACT preparation classes involve all kinds of cost. All these expenses are huge.

So, my response to all this is that, yes, the costs are often a lot for STM trips—as well as many other activities for teenagers. However, what an STM trip can specifically provide is a great opportunity for youth to learn about financial stewardship. Fundraising efforts can teach them so much, especially in that they are raising funds essentially to help others. Moreover, in considering the cost of going on a mission trip versus something more "self-serving," they are beginning to understand stewardship and service as a Christian, and that the Christian life has a different purpose. They can certainly enjoy themselves on a vacation or go on a trip to Disney World. Having fun is great. But they are called to live not only for themselves but for others and those in need. "Missions" is a calling for them as Christians.

Another critique of STM trips and money is that the money can be used for other things—even for supporting long-term missionaries. There are a few ways I try to resolve this dilemma. Year round, our youth group does various fundraising and serves various organizations. For example, we are huge fans of World Vision's 30-Hour Famine. Likewise, we raise money to support the digging of wells in Sudan each spring. As a youth ministry, we are teaching our teens to be financially considerate and responsible not just for STMs but in every area of mission outside of just the "short-term" time period of their trip.

When it comes to the critique that money can be better served supporting the long-term missionaries, my response is to that this support can still happen, especially for long-term missionaries in the STM trip locations you visit. Our youth group intentionally supports and partners with an inner-city church location that we do an STM trip to every year. Likewise, for many of our overseas trips where we have served alongside and with career missionaries, we continue to nurture long-term relationships with them after the trip. We pray for them. More importantly as it relates to the "money" issue, we continue to work with the missionary to ask them how we can financially support them. We will ask them if, for example, they may need a new computer, or video projector, or the cash to purchase something else they need.

Ultimately, there is money involved in any STM trip. However, if considered and thought about carefully in connection to continual and long-term missions, STMs can combat the critique that they are "wasting" money. The money aspect of these STM trips can become just a first step to being good financial stewards and servants long term.

Critique 4: "STM trips don't support those doing long-term ministry in that location." For youth pastors, one potential area of frustration is "drive-thru" parents—parents who just drop off their teens and don't get involved in the youth ministry. In these cases, however, we at least have a great opportunity to minister to their teenagers. Can you imagine the frustration for missionaries who have a mission team come once and never return? Perhaps some career missionaries are used to it. Perhaps others never want us to come back anyway? However, this "come and go" practice of STMs, which does not support missionaries in the field long term, is a major critique of short-term missions.

I know of a local church that has a ministry in Kenya and maintains a long-term relationship with other ministries in Kenya and with Kenyan pastors. They go every year to the same area to build and help the orphanages they have partnered with. When the earthquake in Haiti occurred, I remember visiting many churches and orphanages there, and I heard that many churches in the United States were partnering or adopting churches to support them long term. I found that it was a great initiative and even today, our church continues to support the Haitian pastor we partnered with during our mission trip.

As I mentioned in the last section, continual financial support for any missionary or mission field that you visit is vital and moves STMs away from the "come and go" critique that many lay upon them. Even if you choose an organization to do an STM trip with domestically or overseas, your youth group can support that mission organization year round, not just financially but also through partnership. Have a vision and philosophy that an STM trip will not be just one year or one summer and that's it. Go into your STM trips with the hope and prayer that you can develop long-term partnerships that include annual or bi-annual trips to the same mission location. I am proud that when we partnered with an urban church in our area, we fostered and nurtured a long-term relationship and pledged to return each summer. Likewise, I have sought to purposefully and actively connect them with other churches who can come and serve at their church during other weeks in the summer.

It's true that many mission trips are too short-term focused. There is typically a lack of relationship-building and partnership with the places we go domestically or internationally. For overseas trips, I have a rule of thumb that I will begin a partnership and return to the location at least two more times in subsequent years or every few years. With technology, it's also much easier to keep in contact with missionaries overseas.

One other note about returning to a location, especially in partnership directly with local churches or overseas missionaries: I believe the impact of going once can still be very great, if the STM trip is done well. However, I have seen first-hand that it is of even greater impact to return to that same location in subsequent years. When the same local children see your mission team return, they sense a real empowerment through that love and care. It is easy for any team to go once. But when groups are reunited with people from previous years, there is such a special joy in that. There is much hope for the people there. Likewise, if you have fostered a good relationship with a long-term missionary, there is quite a delight for them when a team returns.

I would add to this one final thought. To combat a "come and go" pitfall of STM trips, consider inviting those you serve with at "their" locations to come visit you (and sponsor their trips). For domestic STM trips, this is much less costly and more readily possible. For our urban church we partner with, we have made sure to invite them to our church often and have done activities with their youth group as well. Moreover, for missionaries overseas, we have fostered relationships that enable them to come visit us. I think this is often a neglected aspect of STM trips and long-term relationship-building.

Critique 5: "STM trips neglect the needs in the local community around us." Another critique of STM trips is that when we go to another location in our country or overseas, we are neglecting our own *local* communities in need. It's understandable that perhaps traveling to another location (even domestically) can seem very romantic and awesome. But this can easily minimize or cause neglect of those with the exact same needs locally.

One way we have solved this is by making our overall program of missions and outreach a holistic one. We use Acts 1:8, which I discussed earlier, as the vision for how we do both. Practically, this means that we are intentional to do outreach to and service for those within our church and local area, another stateside location, and overseas. Our summer mission trips are billed as "one team, three locations." This means that in any given year, our youth do outreach and service work within our church and the local community, mission trips to locations here in the US (domestic mission trips), and STM trips internationally. One team, three locations.

I realize that not all youth groups can do this. Hence, what I would suggest is that your mission and outreach be focused seasonally. In the fall, our church focuses on serving the needs within the church itself. Our youth group gathers for a day of service, which can involve some maintenance work or ministering to the elderly in our congregation. In addition to that fall work *within* our church, we look for spring projects we can do with a slightly expanded reach into our local town or community. For example, during Easter we partner with another church to deliver Easter meals to those in need. In the summer, of course, is when we focus on STM trips—domestic and/or international.

Missions that are just focused on *going* somewhere or are always travel intensive can definitely lead to the neglect of local ministries, even one's own church. Moreover, if missions are just focused on the short-term time period during the summer, the result is often neglect of a missions mindset the rest of the year. STM trips are best incorporated into a year-round effort that can be made locally and in other locations.

Similarly, as far as missions goes, a healthy theology and *teaching* about it is always a great way to move away from the "neglect" of local service and work. In other words, missions need to be expounded upon in small groups, youth talks, Sunday school, etc., to help your youth group and church see it as an everyday commitment. In our youth group, we have made the effort to help our teens see this by having teachers, doctors, lawyers, and even an orchestra conductor (all from within our congregation) come talk to our teens about how they live out their missional faith daily. I have enjoyed this ministry, and it has been a great way for our youth to see that missions are an everyday thing—in their lives and in the daily lives of adult believers too. It's not just a "far away" thing we do on trips.

Critique 6: "STM trips don't offer systemic solutions for the needs of those we are going to serve." Dr. Martin Luther King Jr. said, "True compassion is more than flinging a coin to a beggar. It comes to see that an edifice which produces beggars needs restructuring." For many years, I have been profoundly impacted by this quote and how it relates to my perspective on STMs.

Even just thinking about it in the context of my youth group brings to mind this one vivid illustration: It starts with a picture of a road going up to a mountain and to the top, where there is a sudden cliff where cars can plunge off, especially our own youth group teens. What would one do to fix this problem so people would not go up that road and risk plunging off a cliff with their cars and dying? Would we make signs and post them up? Would we tell people about the cliff? Would we post warnings about the cliff on Facebook?

The proper solution to this cliff would be to make some kind of permanent barricade, so no one could go up the road, right? Or perhaps we would destroy the road and rebuild it to take a detour away from the cliff. Even better, perhaps it would be best to get rid of the road all together, so cars could not go up to the mountaintop at all.

Ultimately, what we see from this illustration is that we would seek a permanent solution for this problem. We wouldn't just seek a solution that would work for a day or week but something to get rid of this dangerous situation forever.

In this way, I understand the critique that STM trips don't often produce long-term solutions to ongoing needs. I understand that many times they seem to only offer a quick one-day or few-days or just plain *temporary* solution. They are not only "short-term" as far as the length of the trip but also in the solutions they offer. In this way, Dr. King was right, especially if you apply the adage to STM mission trips. If we are to truly live out compassion via our STM trips, the trips must be more than just coming and "flinging a coin" to the people we meet and serve. Without considering systemic change or, as Dr. King stated, a "restructuring" of what is causing the need, then whatever we do is only a temporary solution.

As I consider this, I do think about Vacation Bible School (VBS), which I know many youth groups do while on STM trips. Some people will tell you VBS is not offering any kind of longer-term solution. In fact, I know that on some trips, our youth group is just one of a string of many youth groups that come to the same location all summer and do VBS. It is kind of sad when we are leaving an STM trip location and we see another church pull up with the same VBS songs, staging, and T-shirts, ready to do the same kind of program for the week that the community just experienced.

Please hear me. I don't mind doing VBS at all. The two summers after the earthquake in Haiti, it served a great need. We were told by the local Haitian pastor that gathering children to the local churches would be of great help to all the local pastors in order to rebuild his and other congregations, because many children and people were afraid after the earthquake and did not want to come back to church. There was a profound opportunity in Haiti at the time—a nation that practices voodoo—for children to come to know the Lord after such a devastating event as the earthquake. What greater "systemic change" than children coming to know Jesus and becoming followers of Jesus?

Our youth group's second summer in Haiti, I insisted that we do another project, along with VBS. We were fortunate after some due diligence on our part to find a local Haitian pastor who had other work that we could do in addition to VBS. He had started a medical clinic for a community, but due to the weather conditions in Haiti, it was always difficult for patients to come and wait for long periods of time in the sweltering heat. That summer, we worked with the pastor to build a porch roof and waiting area for the medical clinic. It provided long-term aid for a community that would benefit from it long after we left. The Haitian pastor still sends me pictures of people coming to be served by that medical clinic.

Over the years, we have made the intentional shift to be systemically focused on our mission trips. It doesn't mean that we have to just build porches, either. Although I will say we have used this philosophy to construct water tanks in Africa, refurbish schools in Central Asia, and build two schools from the ground up in Brazil and Africa. But like I said, even VBS can be fruitful and important. For example, when we have traveled to Muslim communities locally or internationally, I see what a long-term impact offering VBS can have in a community.

Steve Corbett and Brian Fikkert of the Chalmers Center offer a different angle of what systemic change can mean for STM trips.[6] They use the terms *relief, rehabilitation,* and *development* to enable those who want to serve others well. By their definition, *relief* is more concerned with temporary alleviation of an urgent crisis. In thinking back to Hurricane Katrina many years ago, I remember that some of our youth group teams provided relief by removing trash that had piled high and was becoming unsanitary. *Rehabilitation* on the other hand is something that happens when the "bleeding" stops, and rehabilitation focuses on recovery. But it's also working with local communities to restore those things that were present "pre-crisis." Again, thinking back to our Hurricane Katrina STM trip, some of our team went to restore and repair homes with local homeowners. Finally, *development* is concerned with both helpers and those being helped working in partnership, and it's about empowering those being helped to ultimately fulfill their calling of working and supporting themselves.

This reminded me of our trip to Kenya one year to build water tanks for local schools. However, we were not only building them, but the local communities were empowered with jobs and roles with us. They were the ones continuing to build more water tanks for the community long after we left. This picture of relief, rehabilitation, and development is a helpful way to consider STM as more than just a "one-time" thing. It gives a helpful picture and focus that any STM trip can have. Our youth group trips can be a great opportunity to *educate* those going on these STM trips about the long-term impact of systemic change, and these same trips offer great opportunities to *live out* and *embrace* this kind of effort.

Critique 7: "STM trips are just another box youth workers have to check off because the church leadership says so." Many youth pastors I talk to are in this dilemma. You may have inherited STM trips when you took over the youth group, and it's what the youth group does each summer. Or, like me in my earlier years, you were told that there was a need and "we would like you to go" with a group of teens. However, please remember that any effective STM trips will need to involve the church, church leadership, and senior pastor. And even if asked (forced) to go, the rationale behind such requests is sometimes quite valid.

Most church leaders and congregations see STM trips for teenagers as a good thing. They believe sincerely that it will be helpful. They see that youth group teens may be able to do something that adults can't do. Other times, the reasons are not so valid. I remember many years ago, adults who went on their own STM trip asked our youth group to go along too, because it was too hard or taxing for the adults to do VBS. They simply felt too old, so they asked our youth group to send some teens with them. To be honest, I didn't like their rationale or the way it all came about. It didn't feel like a partnership, it felt like the youth group going and doing what the adults had rejected.

However, as I discussed and outlined in the brief history of youth ministry in the first chapter, just as youth ministry has become a specialized and (I would argue) important part of the church, STM trips can become a specialized and important part of youth ministry. Youth group mission trips have arisen as a natural outpouring of what youth ministry has done effectively. If youth ministries are effective relationally, drawing youth to church, then the fruit of this endeavor will be new believers and disciples.

Consequently, any ministry—let alone youth ministry—would want to foster ways that these disciples can serve Jesus. Hence, missions and STM is a logical way for teens who are growing and maturing in their faith to serve Jesus. I'm going to note Steve Corbett and Brian Fikkert again, who have stated: "A healthy, effective trip is merely one piece of our larger commitment to learning and engagement with what God is doing around the world and in our own communities."[7] Let's see the great opportunity that STM trips can be for our youth ministries and individual teens.

And as I think back to that time our youth group was asked to do VBS because our adults thought it was "too hard," I can see that our teens showed a lot of maturity. They not only served the community that we went to with excellence but we made all the adults on that trip get involved also. We didn't let them sit back. We actually "discipled" them, in a subtle way, to serve Jesus without excuses. As a direct result, in subsequent years, we have had all mission teams from our church—whether a youth group team or an adult team—do VBS training before any mission trip, so that all of us could effectively do ministry for Jesus.

Another emerging paradigm and opportunity that many youth pastors are talking about and nurturing more intentionally are intergenerational mission trips. The hope is that through STM trips that are intergenerational, youth group teens will be more connected to the larger church and have deep connections to the church body. In my own personal doctoral research on innovation, I have encountered youth pastors and churches as they plan STM trips that are intergenerational. They see great fruit from these trips. Because of the relationships built between teenagers and adults, the youth are now less self-absorbed and more focused on others. (And I imagine some adults gain better perspective as well, only by hanging out with teenagers!) They are sharing space together in these mission trips, and that has led to them being more intentional about their relationships and roles in the larger body of the church.

Similarly, many youth pastors say that their churches are now becoming more eager about missions. They have become excited that youth and adults are serving together and see STM trips in a new light. There is new momentum and excitement. Overall, I see intergenerational STM trips as one paradigm for youth pastors to consider as a new, fresh, and innovative way to do missions with their youth. It's an opportunity to make being "forced" to do STM trips into something more fruitful.

Finally, there's one last aspect for youth ministries to consider, and it is fairly obvious. Spending a week or two on an STM trip is probably one of the most powerful ways to develop deep and vibrant relationships with teens. You may be forced or asked to go on an STM. You may have inherited it as a program for your youth group. But I know many youth workers will tell you that spending that time serving with their youth on an STM trip is one of the greatest ways to develop relationships with them. In the end, don't fret, youth workers. STM trips are a great opportunity for you and your youth ministry.

CHAPTER 3 | SO, WHY GO?

I understand the critiques of STM trips. I listed and tried to respond to the most common ones in the last chapter, to show how we can most effectively move away from these critiques. Again, they each have some truth to them. Many of them can cause the STM trip effort to go awry. However, after being a pastor of youth and families for many years, I want to confess again that I really believe in STM trips with youth. I believe in what they can do and how they impact the lives of teenagers. Moreover, I believe that STM trips can be greatly beneficial to those we go to serve. STM trips with youth groups offer a powerful opportunity.

But a biblical and theological understanding of missions and STM is foundational to a trip's success, and the rationale, goals, visions, and purposes for these trips must be built upon this foundation. Additionally, the goals and fruits youth workers would like to see from these STM trips for teenagers must also be considered. If these are not clear, then there will always be criticisms of STM trips (especially with teenagers) and a questioning of why we go in the first place.

FINDING THE PURPOSE

A well-known youth ministry guru and I were having a conversation online. He said to me, "I think I still wrestle with the reality that mission trips have become an outreach tool for unchurched kids because of social justice awareness [when I feel] like they should be reserved for more spiritually grounded students." This echoed some of my struggles with STM trips and the overall purpose of STM trips for youth groups and teenagers. I immediately understood his dilemma. I believe it speaks to a larger theme and question about STM trips with youth groups. What is our ultimate purpose and rationale for them? Why do we go or should we go on STM trips with teenagers despite all the criticisms? In fact, a fellow youth workers who sees my love for STM trips always ask me, "What is your priority: the mission *or* youth ministry?" It's a great question I believe I need to ask myself. Am I going on missions for the sake of mission, which *happens* to be with our youth group teens, or am I taking the youth group teens for the sake of the mission but *also* so that they might learn and grow in faith?

In this chapter, I've outlined a few important reasons to take STM trips with teenagers and youth groups.

Reason 1: Go because God calls us. We go on missions and specifically STMs because God calls us to go. It is clear in the Bible that God calls us to go. I have outlined (and do understand) the critiques and reservations that people have about STMs. I have also offered my responses to them. I strongly feel that all the critiques about STMs can be wisely embraced and that we can navigate through them to make STM trips more viable and efficient. If we believe God calls us to these mission trips, then we can overcome the potential pitfalls. Again, we must never forget that we are ultimately called to go.

Logically speaking, a *short*-term mission trip is the only way we can ever take our youth group into missions. As I noted before, no parent is realistically going to let their high school or middle school student go on a long-term mission trip without them for a few years. That would be crazy. Hence, the STM trip is the only medium for them to go and respond to God's calling. Moreover, with the proper preparation and teaching, the STM trip as part of an overall youth ministry provides teenagers abundant opportunities for growth and service.

Reason 2: Go because with a clear purpose, STM trips are effective. Going back to the dilemma posed by the well-known youth pastor about missions trips as social justice versus "real" mission trips for spiritually mature teens, I would probably say that both/and is the answer to his dilemma. Not that mission trips should be an outreach "event" to unreached teens within your own team. However, if as a ministry you have a solid and clear understanding of what missions and STMs are, then I can say that if unchurched teenagers are being used on your team for God's work, why not?

One notable critique of STM trips in youth groups cites that the spiritual experience often does not go beyond the duration of the trip or have lasting impact. Hence, the critique goes, after an STM experience, teens just return to the same lifestyle and habits as before the trip—they've had no spiritual encounter. If this is true, then the unchurched or less spiritually mature teens would definitely go back to their same lifestyle. However, with a clear purpose and rationale for your STM trip, you can work to move away from this.

I often share with my teens and other pastors that God used a donkey to change Balaam's plans. The Apostle Peter also denied Jesus three times, despite being called to the inner circle of the disciples, and was eventually restored and commissioned to God's work by Jesus in John 21. Youth ministry is about working and loving teenagers who are in the process of developing spiritually. We will have many spiritually grounded teens who are "gung-ho" and fired up for service activities and mission trips, but we will also have teens who doubt, struggle, or may not be ready yet to even come to church. So, does this mean we shouldn't have STM trips because some teens doubt or struggle?

At our youth group, we are clear about our purpose and rationale for missions and STM trips. We teach, educate, process, prepare, and train for our STM trips and have a long-term view of them. The purposes of the mission trips are realized both during the trip and during the preparation for the trip, with a lasting effect that is woven into the hearts and minds of teens. *This is important.* And it's a needed paradigm shift for STM trips with youth.

Admittedly, some teens may not even be Christian. They may be unchurched. They may have the littlest of faith. But our youth ministry is clear about what our mission trips are all about. We have purpose. We are clear that these trips are about more than solving social justice issues or getting community service credits for school.

Knowing that our youth are developing spiritually, we will also screen and educate each person depending on their spiritual maturity level. Our church is fortunate that we can have a few different trips each year. As such, we try to make sure that the more spiritually mature youth go on certain trips. For example, while we go to Central Asia to fix and repair elementary schools and start computer labs for schools in need, we know that the purpose for these trips is to evangelize and share the gospel with Muslims and non-believers. With such a focus, I would hesitate to take a non-Christian/unchurched teen. Rather, I would talk with the parents and require the young person to go on a trip where perhaps something like construction was the focus. I know God would use them and could even work in their lives during that type of trip. In addition, there would be great opportunities to build a relationship with them and teach them about faith and missions while on such a trip.

I know many youth ministries do not have the resources or luxury of multiple mission trips. That was the case in our youth group for many years. Even then, I made the rationale for and purpose of the STM trips to the parents and youth clear. Our missiology was well-defined and whichever stage of maturity teens were at, they knew what mission work was about. Whether it was social-justice-seeking teens or more spiritually mature teens, we diligently prepared and educated all of them about and for the mission trip.

STM trips just don't have to be an "either/or" proposition, as I discussed with that youth worker—only for the spiritually mature or only for the totally unchurched. With limited spiritual maturity in mind, I know many churches and youth groups who have attempted to rename or repackage their STM trips as "vision" trips, "growth" trips, "discovery" trips, "learning" trips, etc., because they worry calling a short trip with (perhaps) spiritually immature teens a "mission" trip might convey some wrong idea of what missions actually is. And I can empathize with this rationale. However, is every

Christian the perfect missionary? If not, why do we need to rename these trips? As I noted from Matthew 28, even right before the Great Commission some of the disciples doubted in the presence of Jesus. Likewise, Peter was restored and recommissioned to serve Jesus in John 21 after denying Jesus three times. I know and have seen many missionaries, even long-term missionaries, struggle or fail in their mission work. There are many variables to any mission work and trip. All we can do is teach our youth what missions is, prepare them for our STM trip and beyond, and go for God's Kingdom work.

Of course, you can rename your trip. Or you can *reframe* your trip by training your teens more holistically for the experience.

Reason 3: Go because youth ministry intersects powerfully with STM trips. The intersection of ministering to teenagers and ministering to others that happens on STM trips provides a unique opportunity for mutual benefit. Taking teenagers, even middle schoolers (because some doubt them), can provide a wonderful ministry blessing to the places we go serve. We all know that teenagers can be adventurous, energetic, passionate, eager, spontaneous, and open. If we do STM trips right, if we prepare and train our youth as best as we can and instill in them a vision and purpose for their STM trip, it can be fruitful and powerful. There is such a beauty in seeing teenagers doing something even as simple as VBS. When I think about the adults in our church telling us to do VBS in a mission field for them, I get a little angry, because teenagers can do so much more. However, I also see that teenagers are so good at VBS! They are valuable, they are loving toward others. They have energy. They are passionate. They are eager. They are open to making new relationships during VBS.

From my own experience and in talking to many other youth workers, we all believe in our youth and have seen them flourish in STM trip settings. Of course, there are some youths who do not. There are some who come without the right preparation and "heart" motives. However, when youth are on an STM trip for the right reason—teenagers who are adventurous, energetic, passionate, eager, spontaneous, and open—and with the right preparation, it is easy to believe that they were created for these STM experiences. If you are a youth worker of any kind, you probably know exactly what I am talking about.

I remember our second trip to Haiti. For the first four days of our work during that trip, our team had to ride three hours to our work site each way, in a school bus with seats for only eight people, on the most bumpy and rough roads, still devastated after the earthquake. As the oldest person (or simply old man) on the team, the youth let me sit on one of the seats, and they also gave up any seats up on the bus for the local Haitian people we were serving with. I can't tell you how sick I was getting, riding on a bus for six hours round trip a day on those bumpy and rough roads. Moreover, I was feeling really terrible for my teens, watching them try to sit back to back—to have some support while sitting on a school bus floor—being bumped and thrown all over the place for six hours each day on that bus. Some were really getting car sick. Some were trying to sleep but could not. There was no air conditioning and it was hot. It was really miserable.

Then recently, I met up with some of those teens, now older, and that Haiti trip came up. We talked about helping to build a hospital. We talked about all the children we met in the area where we were serving. We talked about the Haitian pastor, who woke up at 4:30 a.m. each morning to drive us three hours each way, so we could serve with his team of people. And yes, we talked about those many days of driving. But no one really talks about the car sickness or terrible conditions or sitting on the floor for six hours a day being tossed about. We just talk about the bonding, the adventure, and the memories. We talk about serving with a wonderful pastor. We talk about what a great mission trip it was. I often think this can only happen with teenagers. In fact, my wife and I, who led that team with another youth intern, often reminisce only about those six hours a day on that bus. There is just something about teenagers who are adventurous, energetic, passionate, eager, spontaneous, and open, and what they can do on an STM mission trip, and how it seems they were simply created for these STM experiences.

Reason 4: Go because STM trips provide unique avenues of

learning. Learning styles vary from person to person and the way one teenager learns is different from another. While many of our youth learn by traditional methods such as Sunday school, small groups, or worship gatherings, the STM trips provide unique avenues of learning and growth for teenagers that many pedagogies of teaching and learning speak to. I am going to highlight three.

1. Service Learning. Service learning is an instructional methodology that demonstrates how STM trips can be powerful and have a positive impact in the lives of teenagers.[1] Researchers have long documented that adolescence can often be a time of less interest in school, less motivation, and low self-esteem, which has further negative consequences such as depression and disengagement.[2]

Service learning, where youth participate in organized service and reflect on the service activity in various ways, can be a powerful antidote for the negative experiences of teenagers.[3] An important aspect of service learning is that it should not be confused with mere volunteering and community service.[4] Service learning incorporates pedagogical elements more formally, such as learning objectives, logging of service hours, and other more structured educational components that are reinforced into a curriculum to help the learners. The impact of service learning is that these experiences offer opportunities for addressing community needs while concurrently enhancing teenager's lives.[5]

So, what does all this jargon really mean to youth workers who work with and serve teenagers and take them on STM experiences? It affirms the tremendous impact that service opportunities can have on teenagers. It affirms the value of service learning from a pedagogical perspective. Youth workers understand that teenagers can be nurtured in their faith through STM trips and it can be of great benefit to those being served as well as our teenagers doing that serving. However, service learning as a pedagogy shows us that the *service* aspect of any STM trip must be balanced with the *learning* aspect of it. For those in the church doing STM trips, this learning could happen in mission team preparation, which should be (at minimum) a series of meetings with teens who are going. Based on the idea of service learning, youth workers need to engage their youth deeply in their STM trip preparation.

In discussing the impact of service learning and the future of youth ministry, Jeremy Myers and Mark Jackson—who co-authored the journal piece "The Freedom of a Teenager"—note the importance of these experiences and how they can help young people experience a life of faith that is vibrant.[6] Myers and Jackson also state the strategic uniqueness that Christian communities have to help youth integrate faith perspectives with service to others. As a youth pastor, I'm encouraged by the opportunities that STM trips can have through serving and learning.

2. *Informal and Non-Formal Learning.* Informal versus formal learning theory is also a great support for the positive impact of STM trips. We all probably understand what formal learning is. In the church context, we may think of weekly Sunday school classes. Even small groups could be classified under more formal learning environments. And perhaps even our STM trip preparations would be more formal in their learning context at times. Formal learning usually has specific meeting times and higher levels of accountability, and there are learning goals and outcomes we expect to achieve.

The critique of formal learning contexts is that they are weak. They are carried out and insulated from everyday life. Hence, *informal* learning experiences can buttress formal learning experiences. Informal learning is the learning experience of everyday and unstructured contexts.

A married adult might relate to the difference between the formal learning of a premarital counseling session or class and the informal learning that happens when they finally get married and live together day to day. What this highlights is the power of learning through experience. People are often shaped by life experiences (informal learning) and often hold on to what they learn from them more firmly.

We can teach all we want about a theology of missions, the Great Commission, and the call to serve those in need that the Bible teaches. (It's important to do so, I might add!) We can even do important formal learning activities in our small groups or youth groups. However, we also need informal learning times. For our youth group, I absolutely love the 30-Hour Famine by World Vision for what it teaches our youth about suffering and the need to care for others. It gives teens the informal learning context that a formal context cannot. This may sound like torture, but when we do the 30-hour fasting period, we also go out and do community service. One year, we did an Easter outreach delivering meals to those in need while fasting. Another year, our youth group went to a local mission organization that hosts missionaries from all over the world. We helped prepare dinner for them while fasting. It was quite difficult to bake fresh bread, as well as roll out and cook hundreds of meatballs, while fasting. It was an experience our youth will never forget.

I am convinced that for teenagers in youth groups in local churches, the informal learning and impact of STM trips is a great way to impact their hearts for life. We can formally teach all we want. We can do discipleship all we want. Yet, nothing will impact them quite like being on the mission field. Meeting a person in a rural area of the country stricken by poverty, talking and working with a person from another culture for a week, landing in a foreign country and eating foods one has never seen before—these kinds of informal learning experiences have profound impact.

Non-formal learning contexts and theory can be an effective alternative to informal learning alone. Non-formal learning is described best as a combination of formal and informal learning. There is some structure but there is still room for informal ways to learn. Christian education professor Perry Downs says, "There is great power in non-formal learning. It has enough structure to keep it going in a systematic way but enough freedom to use life experiences for teaching."[7] Non-formal learning has freedom to be responsive to what is happening in the lives of the teens, using experiences for teaching. Perhaps too often, STM trips have lacked this non-formal learning—the combination of formal and informal. Being intentional in our STM team training to have both types of learning experiences is an effective way to aid our youth in processing what they are being taught and what they are seeing. This can be done both during and after the trip, so the lessons of the STM trip experience can be embraced throughout their lives.

3. Learning Through Identity Crisis and Commitment. Finally, there is the aspect of identity crisis as a process of learning that STM trips can provide. Developmental psychologist James Marcia's work related to adolescent development has always been an impetus for me as I have thought about STM trips with youth and his theories on identity crisis. I can probably best help you understand this theory with an example.

Over the years, we have gone to some remote areas of the world, far removed from our teens' daily lives. I remember just a few years ago being in a secluded part of Central Asia and our youth were given some milk to drink. Horse milk, not cow's milk. Horse milk has a very unique and different flavor. Trying new and uncommon foods can cause quite a stir in adolescents. The distinctive taste is one thing. Their reactions and reflections on the taste is another story. It immediately makes them compare these new tastes to foods they have at home—what they miss, what they like, and what is "disgusting" to them.

Outside of new food, just taking teenagers to new environments can have a substantial effect on them. Taking our youth from their suburban community to a rural farming one is quite a shock to many of them—and vice versa. Many urban youth groups also travel to suburban communities for mission trips to give their teens different experiences. That's quite stunning for them as well.

One of my closest friends, who was an urban youth worker, took teenagers from some difficult situations in their urban contexts and brought them overseas to a smaller community in Ireland. Thus, their mission trip was to a more rural setting *and* these teenagers got to travel to a place that they never imagined being able to go to, because of their life circumstances. Hence, they too were experiencing environments and challenges for the first time in their lives that were far different than their own, much like their suburban counterparts would feel dropped into an urban setting. Their mission trips were just as powerful for their group, and how their teenagers experienced Christ through service on a mission trip made a lasting impact on them as it challenged their thinking and faith.

Ultimately, the value and power of such experiences varies. Going back to Marcia, however, there are very relevant theories of identity development and the critical stages of identity crisis and commitment in adolescents.[8] Marcia found there are times in an adolescent's life where values and choices are called into question and reevaluated. This "crisis" is a time of upheaval for the teenager, but often the end result is a time of new commitments and values for the teenager. The final stage of this process is called "identity achievement," where a fresh commitment to a new sense of identity is achieved.

I have seen youth ponder and reflect on their values through STM trip experiences—whether from being exposed to new foods, going to a new country, seeing a poor urban community for the first time, or experiencing the injustices of the world… whether urban or suburban teenagers—and have watched first-hand as new values and commitments arise in their lives.

Reason 5: Go because STM trips foster both missions and discipleship. I have seen the diagram on the following page in various places and it's still encouraging to me.

The wheel is the mission of the church, which symbolizes the church moving forward and doing important things like missions as part of its Kingdom work. Discipleship is the engine, which powers the mission of the church as well as missions in general. For youth ministries, this diagram shows the need, importance, and opportunity for missions and discipleship to co-exist and to develop alongside each other as part of the STM trip. Discipleship is the engine that powers missions, and missions functions in the context of discipleship.

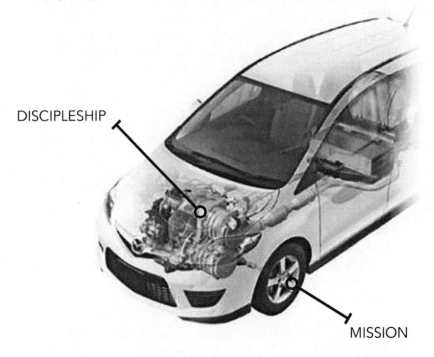

DISCIPLESHIP

MISSION

Over the years, many have critiqued youth ministry of being entertainment- or program-based. I personally don't think all the critiques are fair. Understand I'm a huge advocate for relational youth ministry that often happens in those contexts. However, I also understand the need for discipleship and helping immature Christians and the unchurched into a lifelong faith in Christ. In this way, I see the important value that STM trips can have in regard to discipleship.

In his study of STM trip experiences in youth ministry, Terry Linhart highlights the need for youth workers to be more faithful and effective in STM trips.[9] He suggests that emphasis should be placed on the "transfer of learning" from the STM trip to the conclusion of the trip. He also stresses the importance of integrating the lessons learned from the trip after returning, along with the continual support of adult leaders. I would suggest that these undertakings can be done both before and after as part of the missions-discipleship relationship. In other words, the STM trip can be a great opportunity for missions and discipleship both to take hold in the lives of our youth.

Reason 6: Go because these trips plant seeds and grow roots.
As a youth pastor who has conducted social science research and completed a PhD, I understand that there can be further studies on the effect of STM trips and how they impact long-term missionary service. However, there have been many important and seminal studies regarding the impact of STM trips on teenagers and youth groups, which reflect, ultimately, how powerful these trips are.

Youth workers will often boast about the impact of having a great STM trip. We all believe in the benefits and growth in our teens' lives. Moreover, the Bible uses the illustration of the "harvest" often as well as "seeds, roots, and fruit" in regard to ministry. As noted before, Linhart concluded that to be fully beneficial in the lives of teenagers, there is a need for follow-up and integration of the STM trip effort within the ongoing work of the youth ministry after the trip.[10] But, his ultimate point is that there can be remarkable fruit in teens' lives grown from STM trips. One important follow-up study from the seminal National Survey of Youth and Religion highlighted how teenagers participating in STM trips significantly participated more in civic engagement as well as religiously based volunteer service.[11] These STM trips were said to raise awareness about the needs of others and economic disparity on a global scale, helping youth reinterpret biblical narratives related to social justice and helping solidify their commitment to service.

Studies have also shown how STM trips impact long-term, career missionaries as well as how they impact laypeople to have a heart for missions. They show that there is clearly important value in STM trips. One study showed the main factors in influencing the decision to be a career missionary were interaction with career missionaries, participation in short-term mission trips, and exposure to the world and its needs. This study concluded by saying, "Potential missionaries need as many opportunities as possible to connect with experienced career missionaries. Providing contexts that are positive towards missions and that foster these relational connections seems particularly conducive to the mobilization of future career missionaries."[12] Perhaps it's idealistic to think that our STM trips could produce long-term, career missionaries. However, there are sociological studies that show as STM trips expose teenagers to the things that God is doing around the world and the ways in which he is showing his glory, their potential commitment to long-term missionary service is impacted.

Another study, conducted by the Short-Term Evangelical Missions Ministries (STEM) investigated short-term missionaries over a 10-year time period after their trips.[13] The results of this study showed positive correlation between STM trips and its impact on the participants. Some of the positive impact related to long-term missions perspectives included a significant increase in openness by STM participants toward long-term missionary service and taking steps towards long-term service. In fact, for those who became long-term missionaries or who were leaning towards it, STM trips were the number-one influence on serving long term.

While not every teen who goes on an STM trip will become a long-term missionary, the study by STEM also made it clear that STM trips impact the lives of participants in other ways. These include an increase in time spent in missions-related prayer and financial giving after the STM trip. I can attest that over the years, former youth group teens who have gone on STM trips came back as leaders. Moreover, as their personal lives got more complicated—with jobs, marriage, and children—they had a harder time volunteering, but many of them still helped financially and through prayer.

Ultimately, studies have clearly shown that there is fruit that comes from the root of short-term missions. The impact these trips have is positive, and they serve a great purpose. There is impact on participants' lives as future career missionaries, "senders," supporters, and returners who will go on other STM trips.

SO, ARE YOU CONVINCED?

In this first section, we've gone from a brief theology of missions and STMs, through a history of youth ministry (and the rise of STMs), to critiques of (and responses to) STM trips, and finally in this chapter we've outlined the amazing opportunities STM trips with teenagers can produce. If you are a youth worker who has done STM trips for many years, I hope this chapter supported your case for continuing and encouraged your heart. If you are someone who hasn't been sure about youth STM trips, I hope this has convinced you to take the plunge and GO.

SECTION II
GOING THERE: PREPARING TO GO

CHAPTER 4 ▍ WHERE SHALL WE GO?
CHOOSING A "LOCATION"

So, how do you choose a location for an STM trip? There are many factors that weigh into the decision, and it's far from an exact science or formula. There actually wasn't much to our first ever youth group mission trip. As you may recall from the story in chapter two, the church told me we had a missionary in a certain location, and we needed some energetic people to do Vacation Bible School (VBS) there. So, they asked (told) me to take some youth group teens.

In talking to other youth pastors over the years, this is often the reason why they wound up going on an STM trip with the youth group in the first place. The church asked them to, it was part of the programming of the church/youth group, or the mission department had a need and saw that youth group teens would be "perfect" for it. Please do not fret if this is you as a youth worker. It's the case for many others. However, as this book proposes, there is great purpose for STM trips with teenagers, and youth groups can make the best of these "mandatory" mission situations.

CHOICES, CHOICES
Despite being "asked" to go, I did have some criteria for choosing certain teens for this particular trip, especially since it was an overseas trip to a developing and rural region of that country. I had to consider factors like travel, costs, safety of the youth, and their spiritual maturity, as I realized this trip could get physically and spiritually difficult.

Even though I was *given* a location first, then had to choose certain teens who I thought would be good candidates for the trip, I made the best of it. The next year, when we added a new, second trip for our youth group, I properly thought about *choosing* a location first. Now I had some criteria on which to base my decision. As the years have gone by and we have added and subtracted certain mission trips, there are some important criteria I have developed in evaluating which mission trips to go on.

Here are some of the factors I recommend you consider:

Factor 1: Your Teens Themselves. It's very important to consider where you would like to take your youth group on a mission trip. Of the upmost importance in making this decision is thinking of the actual individuals in your youth ministry and the appropriateness of a trip that best fits your contexts. For example, I would not take immature youth to Central Asia, where the travel can be taxing and where open proselyting or evangelism can get your group in trouble. This is not to say middle school students cannot go on overseas trips. Or, on the other hand, that someone in high school is more mature. In fact, 1 Timothy 4:12 says, "Don't let anyone look down on you because you are young, but set an example for the believers in speech, in conduct, in love, in faith, and in purity." Understanding the maturity of your youth and how their maturity impacts your STM trip decisions, however, is what I want to emphasize here.

Recently, I was talking to a mother about which mission trip would be best for her teenager. Her teenager went on our construction-based trips both years of middle school and loved them. Her desire was that her teenager's third experience be on our local, urban mission trip. This trip was more relationally based, where we led a summer camp during the day and hosted VBS in the evening. It required a level of relational skills, as each teen would be working with little children. In this case, I had to discuss with the mother if her teenager was mature enough to handle these contexts.

In considering both the location and youth, I think about what kind of maturity they will specifically need *physically*, *mentally*, and *spiritually*. I know some youth groups who gladly take *spiritually* mature teens, even middle school students, to overseas locations. Personally, I not only consider the general maturity of teens—as I've explained—but I must deeply consider their *physical* maturity and readiness for certain trips, especially for difficult and harsher overseas locations (again, take the example of Central Asia). Sometimes, the physical demands on a sixth or seventh grader may be more challenging than on a more physically mature, older teenager—think not only about travel but food and eating in a foreign culture.

Over 25 years ago, I took my first STM trip to a very remote village in Mexico. There were no roads, very few buildings, and there was no refrigeration. Because it was such a rural and developing country at the time, everyone (and I mean everyone) got sick. Upset stomachs and diarrhea were rampant. After years of going to the same location, there are now roads, more modern amenities, and appliances/electricity in most of the homes. I would have no problem taking anyone there today, whereas back then, I needed to take into account the physical maturity of each teen. I needed to consider physical health and stamina. Sometimes this meant taking older youth who could handle more physically demanding tasks.

I'm not trying to lessen what middle school students can do. But it does remind me of one of my youth ministry interns who played football on one of the best teams in the area. In high school, he remembers a small, scrawny freshman who got teased and beat down, but this same beleaguered teen now plays in the NFL as an adult. At certain times, a person's physical attributes *do* matter, and there are often great changes in physicality from year to year during adolescence.

In my youth group, finishing tenth grade and turning 16 years old are requirements for going overseas. It has simply worked for *our* church and youth group. In considering the physical maturity of teens, it has been a good guideline. For trips where social interaction and emotional maturity are important, being in at least eighth grade is a requirement for considering teens. These grade and age parameters are not set in stone but do offer guidelines.

When it comes to teens, there are also a few other things that are very important to bear in mind. First, their school calendars. Our teens come from a variety of school districts, and their last day of school can vary by seven to 10 days. If you live in an area of the country where makeup for snow days or other unexpected events may be added at the end of the school year, plan for this. Leave enough time between the end of school and the day you depart for your STM trip. This is tricky because you are planning these trips well in advance. Finally, there may be other competing priorities in your teens' summer breaks. In my area of the country, high schools have athletic training for fall sports as soon as summer breaks begin. Similarly, those in marching band have practice at certain times in the summer. Many SAT/ACT preparation classes occur in the summer. These are all things I consider in an effort to afford as many teens as possible the opportunity to go on an STM trip. But understand that while checking local schedules for these issues is important, it will be impossible to accommodate the calendar of every teen. At some point scheduling conflicts will occur, and it's up to individual families to decide what's best for their teens when that happens. Which brings us to our next determining factor…

Factor 2: The Parents of Your Teens. I understand that with any mission trip, there are risks involved. As a parent of teenagers, I want to know that my children are going on a safe mission trip that will add value to their lives and be a good spiritual experience. Safety plus the educational/spiritual value for their teenagers seem to be the priorities of many parents when decisions to participate are made. Even for non-believing parents or parents who are not as mature in their faith, a worthy social justice and learning experience probably tops their priorities for sending their teenagers on an STM trip.

As a youth pastor, I embrace these desires of parents. Although I must admit that the spiritual growth and the purposeful task of fulfilling God's Great Commission and loving others in need is probably *my* biggest hope for the STM trip. I remember going to Haiti in 2010, a few months after the earthquake. This trip was quite a worry for many parents because of safety concerns as well as the intense heat and lack of water supply. In 2008, we canceled a trip to Kenya because of the potential for volatile situations due to the national elections.

Even in dealing appropriately with apparent safety concerns, anything can happen. In 2013, the same Nairobi market where our team went souvenir shopping was attacked by militant extremists a few weeks after we returned to America. Many people died, and I am very aware that *could* have been our team. A colleague told me about an incident with his youth group and an STM trip in rough part of Los Angeles. They heard nearby gun shots and had to "hit the deck." After this incident, my colleague had to reevaluate this STM trip location and the potential danger it presented. He realized that, though not intentionally, he had put his youth in harm's way. It was not his fault, but some parents felt that way. Finally, in the summer of 2016, our own church youth were slated for a connecting flight through Istanbul, Turkey, and two days prior to our connecting flight home, the airport was attacked by terrorists, shooting and killing innocent bystanders and setting off explosives. Hence, I am praying and discussing with our church and parents how our youth group should proceed with STM trips overseas in the future.

As a youth worker, you cannot alleviate all the safety concerns of every parent. Even as I was writing this book in the early part of 2016, one of our planned STM trips to the Dominican Republic was being re-evaluated due to Zika virus concerns. It's understandable. Moreover, choosing STM trip locations in view of parental considerations, such as safety and solid opportunities for learning and service, will help garner parental support. Yet, there will be parents who still have great fears. There will also be parents who only care about the educational or social justice experience. Considering the concerns of parents may be a secondary reason for choosing a mission trip location, but these concerns (and parents) still need to be respected.

Factor 3: Cost of the Trip. There has been a lot of criticism in recent years regarding the costs for STM trips and the seeming lack of "return on investment" (ROI). In our youth group, we have offered different mission trips at various costs. I realize that not all churches can do this. However, it has been important to propose as many options as possible. This has allowed our youth and families to discuss cost and the amount of time and effort for any fundraising.

We have a local summer mission trip, which partners with an urban church in the city. This is a great opportunity for youth to have a cross-cultural mission experience, because this truly is a different culture from their own, despite being local. And, since it *is* local, the cost is much less than traveling overseas. On the other hand, we also do a trip that is more expensive because of the cost to travel to a rural area of the country, as well as the cost of purchasing tools and supplies. However, it's ultimately less expensive than any international/overseas STM trip. Depending on the location, even overseas travel will vary. Living outside Philadelphia, a three-hour plane ride to Haiti will cost less compared to going to Kenya or Central Asia. Bearing this in mind, I alternate locations for our overseas trips each year, going on trips to either North or Central America one year and then Africa or Asia the next year.

Many churches, including our own, have gone to great lengths to be creative about saving costs. Some churches will identify a local STM trip and find a church to accommodate them while in the mission location. Other churches with a more local mission trip will even return each night to sleep at their own church. While this option may lose some of the luster of a typical STM trip, it can save huge costs. Ultimately, it will take some creative effort to save money on any STM trip. But thankfully we live in a time where we can "google" just about anything, and it's not as difficult to find cost-saving options as it used to be.

Of course, most youth groups I know do fundraising activities to cover the cost of the mission trip. But this is also part of considering a trip and the cost. Fundraising for a trip overseas versus a domestic trip will be quite different. As you plan your mission trip(s), you will need to consider costs, even if your group is fundraising for the whole trip. The higher the cost, the more fundraising (and time) it will take to raise the funds.

But one final word about costs. In my church, we have teens from varying socio-economic situations. During the economic downturn in 2007-2009, it became even more difficult for certain teens to go on an STM trip. I never want finances to be the only reason why someone cannot experience an STM trip. For this reason, I have set up some opportunities for actual financial assistance—not just team fundraising—to lessen the burden of the family/youth portion of the mission trip fees. We have also created ways for these teens to alleviate costs by participating in additional fundraising. Whatever the situation, I try to consider various incomes and have options available so that the cost of a trip will not be the only factor in whether or not a youth can go.

Factor 4: Mission Trip Organization vs. Independent Trip.
Our youth group does mission trips with (1) actual mission trip organizations devoted specifically and entirely to youth group mission trips, (2) trips in partnership with a local, urban church that invites churches like ours to partner with them over the summer, and also (3) trips directly with overseas missionaries—independent of their organizations, working directly with the missionaries themselves. In this sense, we run the gamut of options for trip partnerships. So, how do you choose? There are a lot of things to consider.

There are pros and cons in choosing to work with an outside, professional organization for STM trips. The biggest pro (and con) is the cost. Yes, it is a pro *and* con. You most likely will need to pay some kind of registration/overhead fee per teen and leader who attends. This will probably *not* include the cost for your group to travel to the mission trip location. If I am taking 20 youth and adults on an STM trip and an organization's registration fee is $400 per person, our group is already faced with $8,000 in cost before even considering anything else like plane tickets or other travel costs. That is a substantial amount of money. However, I have found that while this initial fee can be quite high, going with an organization has its pros/benefits. As part of paying to partner with an STM organization, you are most likely going to be able to choose a location that is "prepared" for you. This means that the mission organization has— long before your team has arrived—scouted the location, prepared the local people for your arrival, arranged your accommodations (lodging and meals), and often prepared quite of bit of materials for your week of service.

In our positive experiences with STM trip organizations—and one particular ministry, Reach Missions, for over 15 years—I have seen the value in working together and going with a missions organization. From the time we register to the time we return home after a week of serving, I feel our team has been supported every step of the way. They prepare us even before we register by answering any questions. After registration, the accommodations, directions, materials to prepare or purchase, and a curriculum to spiritually prepare are all sent to us. Before we arrive at our mission trip location, all the things we need—such as paint, ladders, nails, drywall, etc.—are ready for us. The major thing we need to prepare is a list of tools for each participant to bring, which is based on detailed information from the organization.

As adult leaders, we need to do some research on each mission trip organization, and getting referrals (from other youth workers) is always a plus. In my area, I am part of a network of youth pastors. We share about the different organizations and experiences we have had on STM trips. That has been the most helpful way to consider which organization I may partner with. Hearing about the different mission trips and how it was a good or bad fit for a certain youth group is helpful to assess what may be a good fit for our group.

Another con to working with a mission organization is that some may be less detailed, less efficient, or even "penny-pinching." For example, when working with a certain organization, construction materials—such as paint and dry wall—were difficult to come by or ran out, and we were stuck without working materials for a few days. Also, while we don't expect five-star dining, the provision of food for our meals—especially for growing and hungry teenagers—was pretty frugal with another organization.

Another factor in going with a professional mission organization is how much input or flexibility you, as an adult leader, will have as far as working and interacting with your own youth group. This may sound weird, but the degree of flexibility and control will vary with different organizations. You will probably need some input or referrals from others to gain a better understanding of what it will be like with a given organization, as some mission organizations aren't what you might call "self-aware" in this regard. Moreover, the degree to which you have input and leadership of your youth group will fluctuate. For example, some mission organizations will have leaders or hosts for you at their location who are part of their organization. They will not only serve as "orientation leaders" on the first day of your mission trip, but they will be with you in nearly all facets of your trip. They might travel around with you, serve alongside you, lead/facilitate your group's devotional times, and even lead the adult leaders. Other organizations may take a more hands-off approach. They may get you started by orienting you on the first day of the trip and making sure you get off to a good start, after which, much of the input and leadership is up to the adult leaders of your group. In all these cases, however, it is important and most effective to have an open and accessible line of communication with the mission organization who is hosting you.

Another aspect of utilizing an STM trip organization is understanding that there may be numerous groups or churches serving together on that trip, depending on the way the organization works. Therefore, a teen or adult leader from your group may room with your youth group, but during the day when they are serving, be placed randomly into a group with people from other churches. This means that as an adult leader, you wouldn't be working with teens from your ministry or you might be working with just a few of them. It will also mean you will be working with youth from other churches. Having the ability to stick together may be a deal-breaker for some churches.

Speaking of such arrangements, there are definitely pros and cons to this intermingling of groups or churches. One benefit is that teens are challenged to serve outside their own youth group and build relationships with other peers and adults. I actually do value this and see the positive outcomes of teens expanding their circle of relationships. However, not being able to serve alongside and with your own youth group is something an adult leader would have to consider. Some may see it as a lost opportunity to spend time with our own teens and nurture these relationships. Moreover, I have personally found it hard to serve with teens from other youth groups, because I have to develop relational capital with young people I don't even know. They don't know me either, and that deficit can become a big part of the trip.

In the end, there are a rich variety of organizations and trips that will have different levels of involvement with your youth group and other groups. Be meticulous in finding a mission organization that is best suited for you, your youth group, and STM trip. If you ask around, you can find an organization that is best for your group, should you choose to go with a "professional" mission organization.

So, after hearing about the pros and cons of using an official STM organization, let's go back to the other choices.

If your church has commissioned or supports missionaries, this is one of the best ways to find an STM trip location. However, it can take some homework to see if you and the missionary would be a good fit. At my church, missionaries (domestic and abroad) are visiting all the time. When they visit, sometimes they request that STM teams come visit. Other times, especially if it is a possible mission location I think could be good for our youth, I do some research on my own. I attend the missionary's presentation and see for myself if it seems we could help or serve the missionary. Notice how I said *serve* the missionary. I believe that when we are going on a mission trip and have connected with a missionary, our first priority needs to be helping or serving the missionary and their ministry. She or he has been in that mission field since long before we arrive and will remain long after we leave. We need to be mindful of relationships already built and work already done by the missionary and not fall victim to the "come and go" critique of STMs discussed in chapter two.

Take time to talk to the missionary first and just tell them of your interest. Listen to them. Again, just *listen*. They will most likely tell you their needs and heart's desires for their location. They will have suggestions or needs. Or, you may just sense their lack of desire for (or worry about) hosting a group of teenagers. And that's okay too. Still, if willing, your church's own missionaries are a great way to find a mission trip outside of an organization. There is great potential to find a fit that is customizable to your STM goals and the kind of STM work you wish to do with your youth group.

A missionary who served in Kenya identified a need for others to help her visit orphanages she had started and do VBS-type ministry with her. While my youth group would welcome the opportunity to serve in this capacity, I also asked her if there was more labor-focused work that would provide some long-term help for her ministry effort. It doesn't hurt to ask. She told me that they were fundraising to build a school but had a long way to go. Through our conversations, we were able to latch on to her vision and offered to fundraise so we could pay for and help her construct the school's cement foundation and fencing. This first trip occurred in 2004, and even today our youth group picture hangs at the front of the school—their way of honoring our contribution. This small beginning is a great example of working *with* a missionary to accomplish great things for God.

Still, the biggest *pro* of partnering directly with a missionary can also be the *con* of partnering with a missionary. When partnering with missionaries, there is no STM organization cost and you have increased ability to customize a trip with the missionary. It's much like cutting out the "middle man." This is definitely a pro, but remember the STM organization costs ensure your team is set up in the mission field. When going with a missionary directly, the planning typically involves more work for you and the missionary, which may have potential drawbacks. If the missionary is not experienced in hosting a team, your team's experience could be affected. Whether experienced or not in hosting a team, you will need to work with the missionary to ensure that basic things like food, water, accommodations, travel, and what you will be doing (at the very least) is worked out. It will also be critical to iron out any details to "customize" your trip.

If your church does not have missionaries or if partnering with missionaries is not feasible, asking your contacts and especially other churches is a great option. I was able to ask a local church about their ministry in Africa a few years back. My intention was to partner with one of their specific missionaries. What actually happened was that I was introduced to a different ministry in Africa. Nonetheless, it was just like finding our own missionary and turned into a fruitful experience.

With domestic mission trips, not going with a professional STM organization has the same pros and cons as not going with an organization on an international trip. The pros are the cost being lower. The cons are that the planning falls to you and the host community or ministry. You will need to see whether or not your team will be able to customize your mission and work with the needs of the place you are serving with. For our youth group, the contexts for these domestic trips have been predominately with churches that have summer ministry opportunities. I have found, however, that the positive of these domestic trips with churches is that a great opportunity for long term partnerships with the church we are serving with opens up as a result. Ultimately, if you do wind up doing an STM trip with a local ministry, a missionary, or church (domestic or abroad), there is a great opportunity to develop long-term, ongoing partnerships. Similar to a lifelong friendship—because the contact throughout preparation and the mission trip itself is more direct and organic—planning an STM trip personally with such partners can promote a great opportunity for long-term ministry efforts together.

Factor 5: Your Adult Leaders. Most adult leaders outside of paid ministry staff will have to take time off from work to go on an STM trip. This means that choosing a location and date *early* is vital. Furthermore, since they are taking vacation time from work, most likely a one-week STM trip is best for them. Going overseas, especially outside North and South America, involves travel time that often makes an STM trip last longer than one week. Considering the context of your adult leaders' lives when choosing your trip dates will usually affect where you go. Don't forget this crucial step. You need these leaders.

While you might love and value teenagers as their youth worker, no parent will send their teenager on a mission trip without the proper number of adult leaders on your team. You are taking minors on an STM trip after all, so you need to make sure you will have enough adults available as you choose your mission trip. The usual ratio is one adult for every five teens. Most mission trip organizations actually *require* youth groups to bring this amount of adults. Likewise, if you are going on a trip on your own without an organization, this ratio still seems like a good way to figure out how many adults you may need.

Factor 6: The Weather. This may sound like a minor factor in choosing a mission location, but it is something to consider. It will also be important as you prepare for a mission trip. Living near Philadelphia, we have warm and humid summer days. But even this did not prepare me for building homes and fixing homes in a different layer of heat. For example, my first year in Haiti, I had never experienced such oppressive humidity. Even while drinking plenty of water, the physical fatigue our team felt was quite debilitating.

Going on a trip where weather is a factor may require taking youth who are more mature—teens who are resilient and have shown traits in persevering and can tolerate these environments. It's simply something you may need to think about, going back to the first factor discussed. In general, finding the right type of teens for more adverse conditions will make the mission trip more fruitful.

In our youth group, I have volunteered to lead mission trips, particularly overseas, where weather is less of a factor. While it is summer here in North America, when youth ministries do most of their STM trips, it is winter in the Southern Hemisphere. And while many people think of Africa as a place of intense heat and drought, there are places in Africa where it is quite manageable during peak STM trip time for those of us here in the US. In fact, it can get downright cold. Moreover, while Central Asia in the summer can reach oppressively hot temperatures, there are many dry heat regions in this part of the world. So, it will be less stifling in the shade during the day, and it can be quite comfortable at night due to the lack of humidity. Weather is probably a much lower priority in choosing a mission trip location, but it is something you could/should think about.

Factor 7: Kingdom Needs. When choosing an STM trip, reaching situations and places where God's Kingdom needs are the highest and where God is calling us to go should take priority. This can be for evangelism or service projects where God's restoration will be a powerful testimony for his Kingdom. My brother, an orthopedic surgeon, traveled to Haiti—along with other doctors from his hospital—within a week of the devastating 2010 earthquake to help those in need. He shared with me about dealing with the intense heat, difficult hospital/working conditions, and living on Pop Tarts for a week. Yet, his rapid response—and that of the other doctors—served an important Kingdom need during the disaster recovery efforts.

It was a few weeks after his trip that I began to consider taking a team to Haiti. However, we usually begin to plan STM trips 18 months in advance, starting with prayer and careful consideration of locations in which to serve. It was quite a quick turnaround to try to get to Haiti by June of that year. Moreover, the result of the devastating earthquake made the infrastructure in Haiti difficult to assess. Even something basic such as securing flights was challenging. Despite all this, our youth ministry felt a compelling and important need to go to Haiti that summer. We felt God was calling us to meet this Kingdom need, and with his help we made it happen.

Years before that, our youth group did the same after Hurricane Katrina. The people living in that area were a community in need. We felt a strong compulsion to get to that area of the country, because the call for help was so great. With both Hurricane Katrina and the earthquake in Haiti, our youth group was faced with a huge need. They were Kingdom needs. We felt God calling us to a place where the hope of the gospel, through physical and spiritual healing, was needed.

While natural disasters may not happen all the time—and especially in such a way that a youth group can respond—I encourage youth groups to seek out places where they may see Kingdom needs.

Considering how physical and spiritual hope and healing is needed in certain places can be a great rationale for an STM trip. A few years back, our youth group helped a local community ministry. They collected, repaired, and sold bicycles at inexpensive prices or donated them to community children who could not afford them. It was not an earthquake or hurricane, but we felt it was a critical Kingdom need we could help meet.

We also have compassion for those of Muslim faith, and Christians do have a call and commission from Jesus to go and make disciples regardless of current religious and political tensions. In recent years, our youth group has made it a priority to go to certain Muslim countries where we can evangelize and share about Jesus. I admit this does not happen without some risk. We do not take our youth group into dangerous militant, terrorist-dominated regions. However, we have traveled to locations where it is evident the gospel has yet to be preached.

In Muslim-dominated countries, we have presented the gospel in creative and different ways. For example, we have received donated laptops from a large computer software company and have set up computer labs for schools. We are very discreet and covert in talking about our faith on such trips. However, bringing and creating a computer lab in a remote school that is in need has been a wonderful opportunity to share the love of Christ in a Muslim community.

Another way we have done this is through our youth ministry dance team, which teaches and performs Korean cultural dancing. It was amazing how the doors opened up in Hungary, as we shared our Korean culture and dance. The Hungarian people not only enjoyed and embraced our dance, but they would then conversely begin to share and teach us their Hungarian dances. This ultimately led to the building of relationships and being able to share about our faith. This same experience happened in certain Muslim countries. What is amazing is that through this common connection—the teaching of national dances—our youth group has been able to minister to people of the Muslim faith.

Many youth ministries simply do not have this kind of dance team. However, sports ministries, such as teaching American football or running basketball camps, can also have a similar purpose and the same effect for Jesus. Evangelism and sharing about Jesus is a Kingdom need and there are creative ways to go about it.

Factor 8. Your Ultimate Purpose. I think all the factors outlined here in choosing a location converge into the idea of *purpose*. What is the "ultimate purpose" of doing an STM trip? It is not so much the location that matters per se, but as you consider all the factors highlighted in this chapter—the teens, the parents, adult leaders, who you partner with, the weather, and (the most important factor) Kingdom needs—what you are trying to figure out is the ultimate *purpose* of the trip. Working through these factors can, ultimately, help you define that purpose. Where you go is important, but hopefully every decision will reflect the "ultimate purpose" for the STM trip.

CHAPTER 5 | DRIVING THERE

Transportation issues to and from the mission field and while you are on the mission trip are important aspects of planning to consider and prepare for long before you leave. Traveling with a group of teenagers is quite different than with a few adults. Transportation should not be addressed late in the STM trip preparation process. In fact, I believe transportation must be considered when you are deciding where to go serve. For example, when our youth group is going on a mission trip that is construction focused, it takes more effort to coordinate transportation. We not only have to transport ourselves but we also have to take tools with us. As the amount of luggage we pack is greater, our transportation needs (space) grow as well. What is clear is how we travel with a group on a mission trip will take a lot of deliberation.

When you choose to go on a domestic trip (and potentially trips to Mexico or Canada as well, depending on your location), you have to decide if you are going to drive or fly. When we went to do Hurricane Katrina relief in the summer of 2006, it was the first time we took an airplane to a domestic, construction-type mission trip. Until that time, to save costs, to make transporting tools easier, and to foster bonding with our youth group, we drove. But driving over 1,200 miles to the New Orleans area and another 1,200 miles back within our time parameters made flying a much better option. Hence, there are some things to highlight regarding driving versus flying to a mission trip.

While we'll tackle the issues of flying to your location in the next chapter, for now let's take a look at driving.

5 TIPS FOR DRIVING

The decision to drive on a trip may not be as simple as one imagines, if they've never done it. For example, in my experience, driving about 500 miles in a car for a personal or family trip takes about seven to seven and a half hours. This does not include any rest stops. However, if you take into account a group of teens, with rest stops, eating, and bathroom breaks, I would estimate that this same 500-mile trip will now take 10 hours.

Everything changes when you are traveling as a group. In light of that, here are some key issues to consider before choosing to drive your teens and leaders to a location.

1. Consider location and drivers. By law, airline pilots and coach bus drivers have limits as to how many hours in a 24-hour time period they can operate their mode of transportation. The Federal Motor Carrier Safety Administration states that 10 hours is the maximum number of hours someone may drive after eight hours of rest. Just considering that standard of safety, I try to maintain a 10-hour daily (or total) maximum rule for our drivers. Moreover, I make sure that the person sitting in the passenger seat is monitoring the driver to make sure he or she is not falling asleep. (No shot-gun sleeping!)

For my group, driving over 1,200 miles to the New Orleans area would have meant two 10-hour shifts plus another five hours. Even taking into account the cost of the airplane ticket as well as renting vans when we arrived at the New Orleans airport, flying was still the preferred travel mode.

Consider the location of your trip and how far you would need to drive. Remember the 10 hours maximum of driving after eight hours of rest rule and a 10-hour per 500 miles rule when traveling with a group of teens.

2. Consider group size. The size of your group is important too. Each person will need to take their own personal luggage and, depending on the type of STM trip, may need to bring supplies/tools. Factor in if you need to take sleeping bags and pillows as well. Ultimately, this could mean a vast amount of space needed just for personal belongings and supplies. Youth groups sometimes obtain or rent a separate vehicle just for luggage. For this reason, I have developed a relationship with a local company that specializes in rentals of moving vehicles. Since they know we are traveling to do service trips, they provide discounts on rental and mileage rates.

3. Consider renting vehicles. If you need to rent vehicles, such as vans or moving trucks, reserve them early. Determine the pick-up and return times, factoring in your travel agenda and rental company hours. If you are leaving first thing on a Monday, you might need to pick up your vehicle on Saturday sometime, since many aren't open on Sunday. If you are returning on a Friday close to when the rental company closes, you may want to return from your trip earlier in the day to save an extra day's rental. Finally, if you are renting, you need to remind your youth to *keep the rentals clean.* I remember in my early years as a youth pastor, especially if the teens were doing any painting and were not careful, rental vans were ruined and extra costs were incurred.

4. Consider bathroom breaks. It is hard to coordinate the needs of a van full of youth, let alone a bus. During travel, announce to your group when each bathroom break and rest stop will be, especially on longer trips. This can set up expectations for teens, so they don't constantly ask when bathroom stops are.

5. Consider the need for unexpected stops. In cases where the need to go to the bathroom just doesn't line up with preplanned stops, I ask youth to at least *try* to give the driver about a 30-minute warning when they are feeling the urge. Where I live, there are limited rest stops between highway exits. Therefore, 30 minutes can provide enough time to consider some options. There was a situation many years ago, when a teen did not give any warning to one of my adult drivers. It was a young middle school student, and she just said she had to go. She literally could not hold it, and suddenly she just went in her pants. Fortunately, she had a fun and spunky spirit. Because

if she didn't, I could just imagine the embarrassment, as well as my
need to explain to her parents what happened.

Car sickness, flat tires, heavy traffic, wrong turns, etc., can also create
the need for improvisation, so know your route and be flexible when
it comes to things that are out of your control.

A WORD ABOUT THE PLACES YOU STOP

Speaking of stops, I prepare the teens before we go for situations we'll
encounter on the way, like rest stops and how they ought to behave
while we're at one. It's so important for them to be aware of cars in
the parking lot as well as their public behavior. The youth need to be
courteous and thoughtful of other people. For the most part, I think
they are. But some teens can get super loud. Or as teenagers, they
can get rude without even knowing it. Something as simple as eating
lunch at a rest stop with teenage boys, who can easily get bored, can
be interesting. I remember our males getting bored once and deciding
to have a belching contest with each other since there was free soda
at the rest stop. As a leader, I want to coach the teens before as well as
while on the trip about our team being considerate and safe, whether
we have stopped for pizza or for a bathroom break at a rest stop.

At rest stops, as soon as the van is parked and before the teens get
out, we do simple things like pointing out a meeting-up time and
location. These all sound mundane and any decent youth leader
would probably do them, but the STM trip is a different beast. Teens
are excited. They are looking forward to going somewhere to serve.
They are probably happy they have left their parents behind. Hence, I
am cautious and make sure that they all know how long we will stop
at a rest area or any other pit stop.

Finally, it is important to emphasize to the teens to travel around in
groups or at least pairs. Even at a rest stops, some may want to get
extra snacks, buy something, or play a video game. For safety reasons,
you never want them to walk around alone. Likewise, it's always
good to do head counts before you leave the rest stop. It may sound
obvious, but there are so many stories I hear from other youth worker
friends of inadvertently leaving a teenager behind, even on mission

trips, that it's important to mention and spend some time on, which brings us to…

WHETHER DRIVING OR FLYING: HEAD COUNTS (ALWAYS)

I am devoting an entire heading/section to the idea of head counts. As you travel for an STM trip—whether departing for your mission trip, departing from rest stops, having bathroom breaks, boarding an airplane, or as you get off an airplane—make sure to do head counts. This sounds so obvious. But it needs to be mentioned and re-emphasized.

The biggest concern is, of course, leaving teens behind. But our first year going to Kenya—over 13 years ago—the problem wasn't a teen. Somehow, my pastoral intern and the team thought I was in the van as we were leaving for the airport, and they did not make that final head count. Unfortunately, I was in the parking lot, making a phone call to my wife. The van pulled out of the church parking lot without me, and you can imagine the scene: There I was… chasing after the van, running down the street, trying to flag them down… And I never did catch up to them. Fortunately, my wife was on the phone with me still, and since we lived less than a mile from our church, she raced over and we chased down the van before they got onto the highway for the airport.

They almost left me behind. But hearing stories from my fellow youth workers, leaving behind a teen is one of their biggest fears—and when it does happen it becomes one of their biggest mistakes.

As the leader, you can assign other adult leaders to count certain specific teens, you can have teens group up in fours and be accountable for each other, or whatever method of counting you choose. I have not done this on a mission trip (which means I have on other occasions), but you may forget or "lose" someone, as you travel as a group. This is obvious, but again so important: Just make sure you have some sort of system for counting heads and *do it*. No matter how small your team, don't rely on a simple "Is this everyone?" or a glance around. Do the counting.

WHETHER DRIVING OR FLYING: TIME CHANGES

Whether doing domestic or overseas traveling, you will need to remember the time changes. I say this because I have seen people forget to account for this. Our first trip to New Orleans for Hurricane Katrina relief was one such year. We were teamed up with another church, and their leader came from a certain time zone. At the end of the first workday, he told us it was time to pack up and go back to the place we were staying. He was so adamant, despite my objections. Moreover, even though his teens were telling him he had the wrong time and he forgot to change his clock, he kept saying his watch did it automatically. We wound up going back an hour earlier than we were supposed to, and he of course apologized later.

If you travel across multiple time zones, you have to be much more precise with meet-up times and wake-up alarms, etc. You also may deal with jet lag for certain trips. In fact, jet lag may not affect you on one part of the trip, but it may on the other end. It just depends on the person. But it is something to be aware of when traveling, whether by plane or by car.

CHAPTER 6 | FLYING THERE

I love flying. If you ever have seen George Clooney in the movie *Up in the Air*, that is me. In fact, I like all forms of traveling. I like driving. I like flying on airplanes. I am one of those people who likes going to the airport extra early just because I love to travel. Moreover, I like traveling with my wife, especially on overseas flights. She doesn't like plane rides due to travel sickness, which means she won't eat the food on these planes. However, I like the food on the plane, so I get to eat two meals. And since they usually give you a choice on these flights, I get to eat one of each. (I just made myself sound like a terrible spouse, by the way.)

But taking an airplane domestically or overseas for an STM trip is a whole other travel animal, and it's also very different from piling your team in a bus or a van. Since we do at least one STM trip a year where our group is required to fly, I have some experience with this. Before I highlight some things about flying, remember again that going to the airport and taking a flight with a group of teenagers is a huge task. Many of them have never flown before.

A former youth group student of mine is now a middle school teacher. Her school takes students to Colorado each year. She told me that before her school takes students on a trip requiring flying, they actually prepare by *practicing* going to the airport. Then they actually *go* to the airport to *practice* airport procedures. I thought that was brilliant. (Though I'm sure they are limited to the non-secure areas of the airport due to TSA safety regulations.)

10 TIPS FOR FLYING

While my youth group may not actually go to the airport and practice, they are still coached and made aware of what to do at the airport, especially as a group. Later I'll talk more about prepping for airline travel with a group (particularly when it comes to passport management), and I will highlight some aspects of what we need to consider when our youth groups are at the airport and we have commenced our travels. For now, here are some realities our youth group considers when flying as a group:

1. Consider the reality that you are booking tickets for a large group—it's not like buying tickets for a family or a few individuals. First and foremost, it must be done early. It is not easy to reserve a block of seats, even for just 15 people. The earlier it is done, the easier it is to find a group of seats. Additionally, you may want to use a travel agent, which has some costs, but may take out some of the headache for you. There are also some Christian travel agents who provide discounted fees and airfares. In my personal experience, while I have found that their prices may be better, the limited availability of flights with a wide variety of options such as departure and arrival times seems to be an issue.

Alternatively, many airlines have a special reservation system where you can call and book a group of tickets in advance. I have found the best ones are those that have some flexibility. For example, with some airlines, you can hold a block of twenty seats until a certain date. If you end up needing fewer seats, you usually do not have to pay for them if you let the airline know by or before the date you need to provide all the personal information of passengers and pay.

Booking early may also provide you with the best chance for your group to sit together. Believe me, with a group of teenagers, it is always good to sit near them. They can get rowdy. Since it may be the first time flying for many of them, they will simply need you around. I remember one of our teens who was flying for the first time got out of his seat in just his socks to go the bathroom. While I will sometimes take off my shoes while I am seated, I would never walk down the aisle—let alone into the airplane bathroom—in just my socks. When

I asked him why he did not have his sneakers on, he said, "I thought it was just like my house at home." Ultimately, there are many reasons why booking your airline tickets early and sitting together with your group can be important.

2. Consider how you are going to get to the airport on the day of your departure and return to the church on your arrival home. Don't forget this aspect of flying a group to a mission trip location. Getting a group of people with luggage and supplies to and from the airport is not an easy task. In this sense, you are planning two forms of transportation: both driving and flying. Please don't make the mistake of meeting up at the airport. It might seem like the easiest option, but it's actually harder and more likely to cause issues.

3. Consider transportation between the airport and your mission serving site. Similarly, I have found that arranging group ground transportation at our destination airport is not easy. Getting vans at any major airport rental facility is difficult and can be costly. Be aware of this and plan how you are going to go about this. If you need vans, some airports have rental facilities at the airport where the drivers can take a shuttle to the facility. Others are offsite from the airport completely. In all these cases, you will need to consider what the youth group will do as the drivers pick up the vans. Will the group go together? Will they wait at the pick-up area of the airport, and if so, who will supervise them when the adult drivers go to get the vans? What's more, depending on your destination, you and your adult leaders may not be the best/safest drivers for your group. Driving in many foreign cultures is confusing and stressful compared to our relatively calm American streets, and—depending on the country—may not even be legal without an international permit.

4. Consider TSA and individual airport and airline rules for your minors when traveling domestically. The Transportation Security Administration (TSA) website states the following: "TSA does not require children under 18 to provide identification when traveling with a companion within the United States. Contact the airline for questions regarding specific ID requirements for travelers under 18."

While this is true, approaching the TSA security screening line with 15 teenagers and a few adults saying "they are all our companions" has proved to be a little tricky. While there is some cost involved, having each of your youth obtain government issued identification such as a passport (or even the less expensive passport "card") can help with this. Some of your youth will have driver's licenses. Ultimately, I have never had an issue with a minor not being able to fly if they did not have identification because they were a minor. But because having a group of teenagers as my "companion" travelers can be complicated, I now require all of our youth to have picture identification, if possible.

5. Consider any connecting flights carefully and plan accordingly. My advice is to book flights that leave plenty of time for connections. I realize that the prospect of a group of teenagers running wild at the airport for extended periods of time could seem terrifying. But believe me, that is nothing compared to a large group missing a connecting flight. Especially in this day and age, airlines are trying to maximize profits and thus often book to capacity or overbook flights. Hence, if you miss a connecting flight with a group of teenagers, it will be really difficult to get re-booked together as a group. If you use the traditional "one adult for every five teens" ratio, that would be six people at a time who would need to be re-booked if you miss a flight. (And it should go without saying, but never ever leave an unaccompanied minor behind—even if they are late to the gate.) So, consider your itinerary carefully and leave plenty of time between connections.

6. Consider your airline's policies about luggage. Depending on the type of STM trip, you may need every ounce of luggage allowance. You may also need to consider the cost for extra baggage—today, many domestic flights charge for every checked bag and a few even charge for more than one carry-on. For international flights, there are quite a few airlines that will check in your second piece of luggage for free. One helpful hint: There are times when you may have a few extra bags of supplies. If you say you are going on a humanitarian trip, a gate agent may cut you some slack and not charge you for your extra luggage or overweight bags. You can't count on it, but it may happen.

When flying to a location, domestic or overseas, we have our team bring their luggage packed with all their personal belongings to the church a few days before the trip. We weigh each bag and distribute any "group" packing items among the personal luggage (see chapter eight for group packing tips). We identify every piece of luggage by writing numbers on the duct tape we have wrapped around the luggage pieces. For example, if we have a team of 15 people going overseas, and we check in two bags each, our team will have 30 pieces of luggage, numbered 1-30.

This is quite the precision-focused activity. If the baggage weight allowance for an airline is 50 pounds, we add things that we need to take for group needs in each person's bag, until the limit is reached. I would suggest that if your mission department can invest in a good scale, it would be really helpful to you and others planning for such a trip. In our years without a proper scale, we would just use a bathroom scale, have a strong person get on it, weigh themselves, get off the scale, hold the luggage, get back on the scale, and then subtract the difference to get the weight of the luggage.

Sure, this all might sound like overkill. But when you are actually moving and traveling with a group of teenagers, having all this done beforehand will give you peace of mind and save you time at the airport. Checking in with a huge group is time consuming in itself. Hence, we consider and know our weight regulations, do all the packing a few days before, and all the bags are weighed and ready early.

There is always that one teen who wants to add or subtract something from his or her bag last minute, of course. I try to handle it like the Oscars results by keeping the bags (envelopes) sealed until we open them at our destination. But you can be as flexible or un-flexible as you want on this. I am, as you have read, more rigid (or maybe just the most OCD youth worker ever).

7. Consider this reality: When flying overseas, *everyone* needs a passport. Later, I will discuss some step-by-step how-tos related to passports. In our youth group, if adult leaders or teens are going or even thinking about going on an international trip, I ask them to obtain their passports (which is not a quick process anyway) *way* in advance.

8. Consider how much time you need to check in at (and get to) the airport. When traveling alone, TSA suggests getting to the airport two hours early for domestic flights and three hours early for international flights. I know many do not follow this suggestion. However, with a group of teenagers, I like to add at least an hour to those estimates. Of course, this does not include travel time to and from the airport.

With that in mind, try to books flights where departing and arriving times do *not* coincide with rush-hour traffic. I live outside Philadelphia, and it usually takes me 40 minutes to get to the airport from my church. I also know that if I try to go to the airport during rush hour, it can double that time. If possible, I try to schedule mission trip flights early, such as a 9:00 a.m. flight. That way we can leave for the airport at 5:00 a.m., long before rush hour. Or, I schedule a flight that departs in the early afternoon—again, allowing us time travel to the airport after the morning rush hour. This is true for arrivals too. If you can arrive mid-afternoon or later in the evening, the people coming to pick up your team don't have to fight rush-hour traffic to get to the airport.

9. Consider what you would do if there was a flight cancellation. One year, we received a call the morning of the flight saying due to mechanical issues, our flight was cancelled. While the airline booked us on a flight 36 hours later, we had to think about what we were going to do with those 36 hours. Our group had all slept at church the night before the 6:00 a.m. flight. Which meant we were all up at 3:00 a.m., not knowing what to do or how to function for the next 36 hours.

For one STM trip to Kenya one year, our flight left Philadelphia for a connection in Detroit, then Amsterdam, and finally Nairobi, Kenya. Due to a weather delay in Philadelphia, we arrived in Detroit so late that our group of 18 missed our connection to Amsterdam, which meant missing our flight to Kenya. We waited in Detroit for an extra 12 hours to board a flight to Amsterdam, then Dubai, then finally to Kenya. In the end, a 16-hour trip became a 36-hour ordeal. We always pray for safe and undisrupted travels while—at the same time—preparing for the unexpected. It is simply good to be aware that connections can be missed or cancelled and think about what you will do in those situations.

10. Lastly, when arriving home, consider how much time you need to pick up luggage, and inform those picking up your team at the airport to factor in this time. I have never had an issue with a parent getting angry when their teenager was arriving home from a mission trip. But it doesn't hurt to be courteous and remind parents that certain matters need to be handled once the group lands.

A WORD ABOUT AIRPORT PROCEDURES

At the airport, there is some wisdom in having some militaristic precision with your mission team. I wrote at the beginning of the chapter how a former youth group teen, who is now a teacher, takes middle school students to the airport a week before their trips to practice procedures for when they get to the airport on the day of. Perhaps that's overkill, but from the moment your van full of teenagers arrives at the airport—and police officers are telling you to move your car/van quickly from the curb—there is a lot of pressure, and a clock is literally ticking.

So, I've learned a bit over the years and definitely have some recommendations:

Have a system in place. I have a system in place and go over how our team will move luggage from the van, to the curb, to inside the terminal, before we arrive to the airport as part of our preparation. So, when we first arrive, we have a few inside the van unloading, others moving the luggage to the curb, while a few others are in charge of watching over the luggage sitting on the curb (this is an important job by the way).

Pre-print address labels for baggage tags. I have a great travel hack that I will mention several times in this book, because it's so useful for mission trips: Pre-print sheets of address labels at your church office and use them for the airline's baggage tags, instead of painstakingly filling out addresses and phone numbers for every single one. Print a set with your destination address for your journey there and another set with the church address for the journey home. This will be such a timesaver. The labels fit perfectly on airline baggage tags and are legible too.

Keep the vans on standby. After all the luggage is out of the van, we let the van go park or wait somewhere until we are all checked in. We ask them to wait to leave the airport area until we are all checked in, just in case there are any issues like an hours-long delay, flight cancellation, or any other unforeseen reason we might need them.

Check with airline agents in the terminal. While unloading is happening, I like to go into the terminal first and approach a check-in agent and inform them we are a group (a group of teenagers!) and ask if they have any particular instructions for checking in as a group. I also tell them we are doing humanitarian work, because it may get me some extra sympathy. Some airlines will then see a group this large—and of teenagers for that matter—and do a few things that could make this process a little easier. I have found that many airlines will not want a group of teenagers bottlenecking their check-in line or holding the line up. They will tell us as a group to move to the side, and they will devote one agent to checking in our group. (This is where the sympathy for being on a humanitarian trip comes in.) Of course, some airlines will just tell us to stand in the normal check-in line like everyone else. But it doesn't hurt to ask when you first get to the terminal.

Inform the team how to proceed. Once I know how and where we'll be checking in (in the main line or in our own line), I go back out to the curb and give instructions to the group as to how we are to proceed. Now I know where to take our luggage (into the normal line or "private" line) and can give them clear directions.

Hand out passports. Once entering the line, if you are going overseas, you will need to give each person in your group their passport. (I've got some great tips for handling passports, by the way. Keep reading.)

A WORD ABOUT BOARDING PASSES AND BAGGAGE CLAIM TICKETS

This book would be lacking if we didn't discuss boarding passes and the baggage claim tickets you are given when checking your luggage.

When you fly for a mission trip, you almost always have to check in luggage to take necessary tools and materials to work with. We are not allowed to carry on these items. Hence, when arriving at the airport to depart for the flight, as teens and adults check in, each will be given a boarding pass and a baggage claim ticket. From one youth worker to another: *Collect the baggage claim tickets.* They are usually these small little tickets with numbers corresponding to each piece of luggage you check, and are easy to lose. In the off chance the airline loses a person's bag, they are a huge step toward locating luggage. Don't risk your teens losing them.

I've already mentioned how we weigh and pack our bags carefully and number them at the church. We number our bags in part because we keep a list of what supplies and group materials are in which bag. This is in the event a bag gets lost, which we have experienced. It may sound like a lot of work, but it's worth it. You can read more about the group packing and record-keeping system we use in chapter eight—you won't regret putting extra time and care into this process.

As far as boarding passes, I like to collect them whenever possible. However, after checking in, your team will *need* their boarding passes (just the first boarding pass, if you have a connecting flight) along with their passports (if flying overseas—more thoughts on that later in the chapter), to be checked by the TSA agent as they go through the TSA security screening area. After we are through the screening area, I like to collect all boarding passes again until it is time to board. I know this sounds like a lot of work. But perhaps because the "anything that can happen..." adage *has* happened to us, I take this precaution.

A WORD ABOUT YOUR ITINERARY

When flying, despite all the benefits these days of electronic booking and e-ticketing for flights, I carry with me the itinerary—including confirmation code and the ticket number of each individual. You want to be ready for any emergency or ticketing snafu. If there is a weather-related issue, these can come in handy for rebooking flights. You can whip them out for any gate agent trying to rebook your group. Another situation is when you book flights with different airlines. This is often done to save money or get better flight times, but it may cause some mix-ups. So, have a copy of your flight information ready.

Finally, on overseas trips where language may be a barrier, pulling out all your confirmation numbers for a gate agent in this way can be very helpful if you have any flight issues. (Perhaps you can tell from my words that these situations are not made up but have all happened to me at one time or another.) Something as simple as having the itinerary, confirmation code, and ticket number of each individual readily available is so handy in those moments.

10 TIPS FOR INTERNATIONAL FLIGHTS

When flying internationally, remember you need passports, you may need visas, and going through customs is inevitable. If you've never flown overseas yourself, this may sound daunting, but there are a lot of things you can be aware of or do in your planning process that will make international travel smoother for you and your team.

1. Inform parents in the fall before the trip to obtain passports for their teenagers. As summer approaches, the passport making process takes longer as many people are preparing for their summer trips. For some countries, you also need to get an entry visa to get into that country before you depart for your trip. Hence, you may need to mail in passports to a country's embassy two months before a trip. In these cases, having passports ready *early* is vital. If you are wondering if you need a travel visa to a certain country, just find the website for that country's embassy here in the US. It will most likely have all the information about travel and entry visas for that country. (Note: If any of your teens don't have US citizenship, not only will they need an appropriate passport from their country of citizenship but they may have visa and important travel document requirements that differ from the rest of your group. Get information on these needs from official agencies well in advance of your trip.)

2. Make sure to check passports of every team member at the *beginning* of the mission trip planning process to be sure they have obtained them, they are not expired (or even about to expire), and that they contain at least four clean pages. One year, I took for granted a teen who was just a fabulous and trustworthy person. I just assumed her passport was good. Somehow I forgot to ask, and on the Friday before a Sunday departure, she realized her passport had expired. I was horrified.

If you live near a government passport agency and it's an absolutely emergency, they can make an emergency passport for you in one day. But this should never be your scenario (although somehow, even a mission junkie like me has had to take parents and teens a few times for this over the years). Some foreign countries will not accept a passport if it is going to expire in a few months or the same year of your trip. Likewise, if you don't have enough clean pages to stamp entry and exit visas, they may also deny you admission. Please believe me on these little things. I have heard it happen to others, so I practice not making the same mistakes.

3. Make sure to make copies of each person's passport. In case of any emergencies also, leave a set of these copies with someone responsible at home. I also take a set with me and usually give a set to one or more responsible adults on a trip with me. There are multiple reasons to get the copies, not the least of which is number four...

4. Make sure when booking airline tickets that you have the exact spelling of names as they appear on the passports themselves. You may think being one letter off is no big deal but it is. Especially with electronic ticketing. If your e-ticket does not match your passport exactly, it can cause major trouble or delays. These days, you also need the gender and birthday of the passenger to book tickets. Don't guess or assume the church database info is correct. Book the tickets with care, check the tickets for correct spellings once they are booked (that very day!)—and for that matter, be sure to double check that every traveler's ticket *was* booked. Being even just one ticket short is a nightmare—and it's happened.

5. Know how to handle passports on your journey. You have to be able to prioritize not losing passports while traveling. Now, let me reiterate the suggestion that you should make a copy of everyone's passport and give them to another adult member to hold during the trip, as well as leave a copy of everyone's passport with someone at home.

While I love and trust teenagers, these passports are so vital to a trip. I think it's prudent to have one adult leader hold on to all the passports when they are not needed. Also, in some foreign locations, for safety reasons, you often need to have your passports with you wherever you are. As a group, I would again have one really responsible adult leader carry everyone's passports.

You definitely need passports when checking in for flights. You also need it when passing through the TSA security screening lines. However, once you get through that area when departing from the US, you rarely need them. (Though in some other countries you may.) Hence, I would collect them.

In past experiences, I recall a teen who kept his passport and had it in his backpack. Subsequently, he misplaced his backpack while in a store to get snacks before the flight. You can survive an overseas mission trip without a backpack and snacks. In addition, even without that passport, you may be able to get on a plane because you already passed the TSA security line. However, you are going to have difficulty getting into the destination country, let alone back into the US.

I recall another trip to Kenya where we transferred flights in Amsterdam. While we tell our group to make sure they have their passports, one teen left her passport in her front seat pocket on the plane. Waiting until everyone de-boarded the plane and getting clearance to go back on the plane was extremely time consuming and difficult.

Heed my words then: Collect passports (and boarding passes too, as I've mentioned) when they are not necessary. Remind your team at other times—if they are required to hold on to them—to double check that they have them at all times.

When heading back home to America, depending on where you are returning from, you and your team may need your passports a lot more than when you left. I have transferred flights in European countries to return to America, and they seem to check passports and boarding passes every time you get on a plane, even if you have already cleared their security lines. Finally, each teen will need their passports when they arrive back to America and will be filling out a customs form.[1] (More on those to come.)

6. Organize the passports when you are traveling. So, hopefully I've convinced you to hang on to your group's passports as much as you can. But if you have ever tried to pass out multiple passports, opening each one to find their names in small print, while trying to hold on to all the other ones, you'll know you need to be an octopus to do it effectively. In trying to handle a group of passports, one of my seminary professors did something really simple but really helpful. He put a label on the back of each passport, with each person's name on it. This made it so much easier. And it won't affect the passport in any way. You may want to check with parents before adding anything that can't be removed, but sticking a label on the back of each passport—even if it's just a Post-it note—can help you in this important task.

7. Obtain notarized travel permission forms from parents for all minors. Many countries, like the US, *can* refuse to allow a minor to cross borders with a non-parent if the proper (notarized) permission form isn't with you. The form would state that the minor is allowed to travel with the church and church leader, without the parents. Not all airlines enforce this domestically or with places like Mexico and Canada, but some will. And with any international travel, you run the risk of having to produce this kind of permission.

Typically this is to prevent child abduction, but sometimes there are other concerns at play. About a decade ago, when traveling to Mexico for an STM trip, traveling with teenagers became complicated because there was a large influx of college (and even high school) students on spring break. Due to the binge drinking, sexual assaults, and disorderly drunkenness epidemic during that time, some airlines required notarized parental permission forms to fly to Mexico. We had fortunately arrived to the airport early that year. Parents had just enough time to get to the airport and sign permission forms in front of the gate agents. In future years, I made sure to call the airline in advance to see if we needed any parental permission. Now, while most airlines do not require this—particularly for travel within the US—it is something good to remember, research, and prepare for properly.

8. Prepare your group for filling out customs forms, visa entry forms, and any other entry documents. Many foreign countries will have some sort of entry document that needs to be filled out—a customs form or other similar document—on the plane or in the airport immediately after landing. This form will likely require the traveler's passport number, name, usually the flight number, and often an address of the final location. You will also have to do a US customs form when entering back *into* the United States. Here are a few things you should consider:

> **Use blue or black ink.** When filling out any form while entering a country, even when you are returning back into the US, blue or black ink should be used. Some teens write in pencil or red ink, which is frowned upon in many other places in the world. Most airlines have pens if you need them, but it can't hurt to be prepared.

Pre-print address label sheets. Yes, we're back to those handy pre-printed labels and yet another way to use them. Instead of trying to tell a group of teens on a plane the address of your destination for these forms—which could pose some safety concerns—I highly recommend travelling with pre-printed sheets of church *and* mission location address labels that you can hand out to your teens in key moments like this. (I discussed these labels earlier and I will remind you of them again in chapter eight. This hack has saved me so much time and hassle!)

Pass out passports briefly or fill out forms together. When it comes to the passport numbers for forms, you want to choose how to proceed, especially if you are heeding my earlier words and have collected all the passports. You can try to pass out all the passports on the plane again or you can all de-plane, go to the arrival area, and fill out the forms together. I like to do the latter because despite all the instructions you give, you can never give teenagers enough preparation about entering into a foreign country and filling out that entry form, and they probably have never done anything like it before. They will have questions.

Watch your dates. Finally, while we Americans usually fill out dates as the month, date, and year, many countries do it differently. For example, July 3, 2015, is written here as 7/3/15. However, outside the US, they often go by day first, *then* month, and year. Hence, July 3, 2015, would be written as 3/7/15. (In other words, when writing dates this way, think of it as the "third of July" rather than "July third.") If dates are written incorrectly, some immigration agents may hassle you about it.

Prep your team to know what to declare. You may also have to "declare" certain purchases from overseas upon re-entry to the US, and what is allowed may depend on the country involved. Do some research ahead of time to be current on guidelines and prepare your group with that knowledge too. Above all else, never lie on these forms. It should go without saying, but I'll say it anyway.

9. Prepare your group for appropriate behavior in customs.
Standing in line in customs is not a good time to have to explain that taking photos (in many airport customs areas), talking about certain things (jokes about drugs and bombs), and being disrespectful to customs agents is unacceptable. If you've never gone through customs, just know it's much like going through a TSA checkpoint… only on steroids. A walk through customs can be smooth sailing or a youth worker's nightmare, and it often comes down to how your group handle themselves.

10. Know the foreign currency. Be aware of foreign currency exchange rates and where to get the best exchange rates when traveling overseas. I would ask the local missionary or host when going overseas as they probably know where to get the best rate. In certain countries, be aware that it is difficult to exchange bills smaller than $100. Likewise, changing back to US currency may be difficult outside the airport on your return trip. One last thing, when traveling overseas to a missionary or host, ask them if local vendors prefer US dollars or not. Sometimes, having US dollars actually is more convenient for them.

CONNECTING FLIGHTS AND DELAYED ARRIVALS

Connection flight times for international travel are a huge consideration. A simple trip to Haiti from practically any US city will often connect through Miami. *Going* to Haiti, this stop is not as much of a factor. When *returning* from Haiti and connecting in Miami, however, the Miami airport will be your first place of entry into the United States. Everyone will need to fill out custom forms, retrieve luggage, go through customs, and re-check baggage with the airline. Then, you will need to find the terminal for your connecting flight and go through the TSA security screening process all over again. This is not a big deal for one or two people. But when traveling with a group of teenagers, it is much more time consuming.

I like at least three hours between connections on international flights returning to the US. There will be times when 90-minute connection times are offered. The airline or travel agents may tell you that this is plenty of time and "within the official connection time parameters of the TSA." This may be true, but when traveling with a group, 90 minutes is often a very small window. (Think bathroom trips, snack needs, counting heads, the inevitable "slowpokes," etc.)

Related to this, boarding times at overseas airports tend to be closer to an hour before a flight and there are sometimes more security clearances at certain airports. I cannot reiterate enough that you should leave your group *plenty* of time for connections.

Along those same lines, if your home airport is your first stop in the US from an international flight, the time from landing to leaving the airport can be extensive. You will have to go through customs and that can be time-consuming for a large group. Plan on being flexible and ask those who are picking you up to be flexible as well.

CHAPTER 7 | A LEADER'S PREPARATION
PT. 1: PLANNING

To quote Paul Borthwick again: "The success of a service project, mission trip, or even a work day is often determined before the van leaves the church parking lot or the plane takes off."[1]

As the youth pastor, youth worker, youth volunteer, or in whatever capacity we serve as an adult leader for an STM trip with teenagers, we are ultimately responsible for the trip and, in particular, for the teenagers. We are taking other people's children, which is a huge responsibility in and of itself. These parents are trusting us with their children for the duration of the trip. However, as we know, the first day of the mission *trip* is actually not the first day of the mission.

This chapter will outline different aspects of what a leader can (and needs to) prepare before going. We've already touched on the need to think through each aspect of the trip in order to have a purposeful and effective STM experience (particularly as we walked through common critiques in chapter two). But now let's go deeper into the details of that prep work.

FIRST THINGS FIRST: LOCATION, DATES, TRAVEL, VISION

I can't say it enough. Everything a leader prepares for in order to have a great STM trip, should be done as early as possible. Picking a location and dates, considering travel options, even (most importantly) laying out your youth group's purposes and vision for the STM trip needs to be done early. Airline tickets, van rentals, and connecting with organizations, these things all need to be done early. As you know by now, I suggest taking at least 18 months to prepare, starting with prayer and considering possible mission trip locations and their fit for your youth group. I understand that this isn't possible for many who do youth ministry. Let me just say again, however, the earlier the leader prepares, the better.

You have read through my extensive tips for planning STM trip travel, so it should come as no surprise that I believe your travel plans deserve a great deal of forethought and consideration. Planning your travel well frees you during the trip to focus on what you are there to do: ministry and service.

SUPPORTING THOSE ALREADY THERE

As a leader prepares for an STM trip, I think one of the most important ideals and values of STMs should be to support those already there, who will be there long after we leave. This means, whether an STM trip is domestic or international, we need to consider the local organizations, hosts, or churches welcoming and hosting us. It means that the ministry considerations of the long-term missionaries we visit overseas are the priority. It means we need to consider the local pastors already doing ministry in the places we visit.

Early on in the mission trip preparation, if you have not done so already, reach out to the hosts, the local leaders, and the missionaries. Ask them their needs and hopes. Tell them you are going to serve and help *their* ministry. There is nothing more "ugly" than going on an STM trip thinking we are the main missionaries. We are doing service and missions, but we need to acknowledge that we are going to *support* and *serve alongside* those already there.

When going anywhere, I try to bring plenty of "stuff." I try to bring extra (culturally appropriate) toys if we know we are going to be doing VBS or extra tools if we are doing construction. As soon as we arrive, however, we let the missionaies know that we are there to support them. We ask our hosts to give our team *instructions* on what to do with the things we have brought. We ask them how they want us to do the VBS and if there are any special instructions. We tell our hosts that we have extra toys and ask how they want to distribute them or that we will be leaving the extra tools behind, for them to use or give away as needed. In fact, our rule is we do not give out *anything* without asking the host first. Not even a piece of candy. We don't even smile at people first. (Just kidding.) However, I believe it is better to let the local hosts do all the "giving away" or at least ask them first, so that the focus remains on the local ministries and not on our team. Looking like the saviors or heroes is not our goal.

BUDGETS

Your STM mission trip budget will vary church to church. In my experience, each team usually has expenses for these STM trips that are the responsibility of each team member and other expenses that fall to the whole team. Some churches will support certain aspects of the STM trip, for example, from the mission committee budget.

In regard to budgets, here are some general things to consider:

Church subsidies: It is important to determine early on how *much* one's church and *what* one's church will subsidize for the STM trip. Some churches have no budget and no supplies, and the team is required to do all the fundraising and supplying for the STM trip.

If you go on a trip with a mission organization, they will almost always require some kind of initial deposit per attendee up front, as well as payments for each participant (at the very least) a few months in advance. It is important to consider who will pay and how to pay for these upfront costs. I know some churches have money or credit cards to cover the cost of things that need to be paid early. The youth pastor puts it on his/her church credit card and has faith that the money will come in. When teens are fundraising the majority of the cost of the trip and money is needed up front for things, it is helpful to understand how *much* the church can financially help and *when*.

If flying, it is a must to reserve and pay for airline tickets early. For example, if your STM trip requires you to purchase an airline ticket for $1000 a few months ahead of time (for an overseas trip) and your group is still doing fundraising, how will you purchase the necessary tickets early enough and who will pay for them? Where will these funds come from? Perhaps parents can cover these fees while youth continue to fundraise to pay for the trip. You can come up with your own system, but this upfront money is something you have to think about.

Frankly, I am so passionate about this "upfront" money thing because our churches often think youth workers have all this petty cash or don't mind running up huge bills on their personal credit cards (a risky move, to be sure). It would be great if churches could support the youth group and youth pastor and be willing to help with some of the upfront costs. A youth worker friend told me that a few years back, a teen was committed to a trip, was participating in fundraising, but then dropped out. The youth was about $500 short of his or her fundraising goal and my youth worker friend had paid for the teenager's upfront costs. It's precisely a difficult situation like this that can hopefully be avoided with some planning and clear expectations in regard to budgets and finances for mission trips.

Youth worker/adult leaders: Expounding on those subsidies, determine who will pay for you and other adult leaders. As a paid, full-time youth worker, it is part of my job to do STM mission trips. Hence, I do request that my trip be part of the overall church or youth or mission department budget. If you are a volunteer youth worker or adult leader, it will probably vary or more likely not be included in a church budget. In my opinion, due the age of the youth we are taking on these STM trips, there is a requirement and absolute need for adult oversight. Hence, at my church, we have made great efforts to partially or fully subsidize adult leaders. As I consider my adult volunteers, I know that most of them are giving up vacation days and potentially some amount of salary to come on an STM trip. For them to incur more out-of-pocket cost seems unfair. Consider your adult volunteers as you prepare a budget.

Transportation: Costs of travel must be budgeted into your STM trip expenses for each individual and the team. On domestic trips, our church rents multiple 15-passenger vans as well as a truck to haul our luggage and equipment. This can cost over a few thousand dollars. This must be taken into account when developing the budget and how it will be paid for.

On trips where you are flying somewhere, the budget needs to include transportation when you land at the airport as well as when you go back to the airport from the mission site. Likewise, the daily cost of traveling at the mission site must be considered. In this way, I have found that going with a mission organization is helpful on overseas trips. Almost all of them take the transportation costs from and back to the airport into account as part of the team registration or individual cost they charge.

Transportation of baggage: Add this to your airfare and consider your expected volume with ground transportation as well. While I highlighted this in the previous chapter, this is just a reminder that baggage costs must be worked out as part of the budget. Either plan for more van space (if you are renting some kind of vehicle), take a luggage truck, or (in the case of flying) budget for the cost to check (extra) baggage.

Food: Don't forget this crucial budget item. Teenagers have growing appetites (as we all know), and when going on a trip, I think it is important to account for this. Most trips, whether going with an organization or on your own, account for meals as part of the cost. You have probably planned for this sort of expense before with day trips to the snow or other youth events that last longer than just a few hours. With teenagers, I like to factor in the costs of extra snacks. Sometimes you can just budget for this and buy the snacks for the team. Of course, this can be done individually. Each person can just bring snacks for themselves. I like to do this more corporately. I have each team member buy some snacks for the group. Usually, we ask each youth to bring Rice Krispies treats, nut packs, jerky, or Pop Tarts that can serve the whole group.

Lodging: If accommodations won't be a church floor or other free option, you'll need to budget accordingly. Part of going with a mission organization is that they usually will have taken care of the costs for (and location of) lodging from your arrival day to your departure day. However, there are times when my group or my friends' groups have gone on an STM mission trip and have had to leave a day earlier (due to travel considerations) or return a day later. In these cases, you may have to think about lodging accommodations and costs.

I know I have hosted other church youth groups at our church who needed a place to stay one extra night at the end of their mission trip while (or before) traveling home. And in my trips overseas, sometimes we would arrive in the foreign country late at night, so we would have to sleep somewhere close to the airport before traveling to our mission site the next day. I have had to arrange for accommodations in these situations. Sometimes you can find free options and sometimes you may need to pay. In my years going to Kenya, we always arrived late at night. It would be difficult to travel further so late at night to get to our mission trip location, which was a five-hour bus ride away. So, from our first year we went, we found accommodations at a Catholic hostel, which involved budgeting for one night's stay. Likewise, even when we are staying at a church (actually, especially if we are staying at a church) as their guests, I like to budget for a love offering to give them. Moreover, even if it is a "free" option at someone's home, while you may not need to spend money, a small gift (like a mission team t-shirt and a thank-you card from the team) goes a long way to show thanks and appreciation.

FUNDRAISING

In conjunction with budgets, you will need to prepare and consider how you will do fundraising and how much each individual will need to raise. I know that with the majority of youth worker friends I have, the reality is that churches do not really subsidize any of the costs of the STM mission trips. On a personal note, I think this is silly, and if your church has a mission department or outreach department, try to work with them to at least support some portion of the STM trip. But the bottom line is that fundraising—to whatever extent it is required—is an inevitable part of STM trip preparation.

I won't speak about *all* the types of fundraising events or ideas you can do, but I would say talk to other youth pastors about your ideas and to get ideas you haven't even heard of. I have learned so much from others about what kind of fundraisers to do. It also probably requires understanding your church and local contexts. One youth worker friend of mine came from the Midwest, where they sold mulch as a fundraising activity. He tried it in our area but realized that most people just pay someone to do it for them.

There are many other fundraising ideas, of course, but much to consider with each. Youth workers will tell you that car washes are easy as far as overhead. But, of course, they take a great amount of time and effort. (And there is a high probability of getting drenched by your teens.) I have always found that food sales work well. Youth worker friends of mine have hosted spaghetti dinners, bake sales, breakfasts, dinners, and boxed dinners that they take pre-orders for. Everyone eats, which often makes food fundraisers successful. Our church opens up two Wednesday nights a year, and our youth group sells dinner and drink items to our church and community. Food does take a lot of overhead. But what I have found is that asking parents to donate a few things that are part of the dinner is a great idea. For a spaghetti dinner, for example, if a few parents donate sauce, a few donate pasta, and other parents donate salads and bread, you can pull off the dinner at little or no cost. Then all the profit goes to your STM team.

Again, I encourage you to work with other youth pastors and get ideas. I have not done this yet, but a youth worker friend down the street gave me the idea of putting envelopes in the hall of the church foyer. Each envelope would indicate a different amount, ranging from $10 to $200. Adults of your church walk by, take the envelope that fits their budget, and donate according to what they can give, based on the envelope they take. I love this idea.

Another aspect of fundraising for an STM trip is doing it individually or corporately. Will all funds go into a "pot" and be divided? Or will each person just be responsible for their own funds by writing letters, asking relatives, and even having parents support them? Whether or not fundraising will be a corporate or individual process must be clear.

HEALTH AND HEALTH INSURANCE

It is important to have the health insurance information for each participant in order. Every once in a while, a teen (or adult leader) will have a health issue that requires a hospital visit while on our trip. We have had youth taken to the emergency room for heat exhaustion and even stepping on a nail. Many missions organizations that have a construction element ask about tetanus shot information in case of emergencies.

In addition to this, if traveling overseas, go to the Center for Disease Control and Prevention's website and see if your team may need any vaccines or special medications.[2] There have been years that we traveled to certain countries and certain vaccines were needed. But don't forget, vaccines can be costly. It must be something you think about and find out early to include in the cost of the STM trip. In my years of traveling overseas, probably the most recommended medication is malaria pills. We took them when going to Africa, South America, and places in the Caribbean. Moreover, even malaria pills have a wide range of dosages and costs. The "daily" pills that can be taken for about 40 days before, during, and after the trip are the least expensive. But it can be a challenge for the youth to continue taking them after they return. There are other malaria pills that only need to be taken once a week for a few weeks, but they cost a lot more.

DOCUMENTING THE TRIP

More than estimating the cost, it is important to prepare and consider how you are going to document this trip for your youth group and church. In considering that, you will need to think about what forum you will use to communicate about your trip when you return. For example, if you know you are going to make a highlight video after you return, you need to focus on documenting the trip with a video camera (or a few). If you are going to do a mission trip report or presentation using a PowerPoint "slide" show), you may need people to take a lot of pictures.

Even a few years back, to document a mission trip, you would need to budget for rolls of camera film, the cost to develop pictures after the trip, and mini-DV tapes for the video camera. Today, in our high-tech age, the cost of documenting a trip, especially for mission reports to the church after we return, is far less. Almost everything is digital. You may need to purchase a few memory cards, but securing some decent video cameras or digital cameras is probably the most you will need. And most churches already have at least one or both. Our church still likes to develop a few pictures for our church walls/ bulletin boards to display after each trip, and that may add some minimal costs to the trip later.

Another important consideration is *who* is going to be part of the documentation process for/during the trip. It raises the question of youth and tech/media devices on the trip. I will discuss this topic in depth later. While I tell our teens not to take cell phones on missions, the youth (and their parents) sometimes complain, arguing they needed them just to take pictures. (You will need to make decisions in this regard.)

Finally, in any location, whether you go overseas or have a trip domestically, it is important to be sensitive when taking pictures and videos. Youth, if they all have their cameras, should be made aware of this too. I suggest asking permission (from your host pastor/ missionary/etc.) before taking pictures or videos of people you meet on the mission field. Likewise, so as to not to appear like tourists on a vacation, it is important to be sensitive to those you are taking pictures of/with. They are not objects, but they are people after all.

DON'T FORGET...

Busy youth workers can easily overlook this important detail as they prepare a group of teens for a trip: If no one will be at home while you are on an STM trip, you need to make proper arrangements. Since my wife has been going on STM trips with me and our children stay with relatives if we both go, I also prepare my home. My three things that I can't forget are:

1. Mail being held at the post office
2. My pets and who will care for them
3. The thermostats at my house

These are simple steps that are often neglected, so this is just a reminder to think of these things before leaving for the STM trip. It all sounds obvious, but when you are trying to get a group of teenagers prepared for a mission trip, preparing your personal life properly can be forgotten.

CHAPTER 8 | A LEADER'S PREPARATION
PT. 2: PACKING

There are things the leader of the mission team needs to prepare for and bring on the STM trip for the group. There are items that youth and adult leaders need to bring personally as well. It is obvious to me then that there are two kinds of packing lists leaders need to prepare: a packing list of things that are needed *for the group* and a personal packing list *for each person*.

PREPARING A GROUP PACKING LIST

Group packing refers to everything we need to take as a team for our STM. When flying domestically or overseas, this gets difficult because you cannot just throw your supplies into a few duffel bags or boxes like you can when you are travelling by van. It takes careful planning, as I've alluded to already.

One huge tip here is that as you consider and pack group materials, you can distribute them to all the different team members who should have extra room in their personal luggage (to help save money on baggage fees). We also document what group things we put into each person's luggage, in case it's lost or stolen. This lets us know what we are missing from our group supplies. One year, traveling to an overseas location, we were going to make pinwheels for VBS and play dodgeball. We had put straws and dodgeballs in a few different team member's bags. When one of the teen's luggage was lost, we knew exactly how many straws and dodgeballs we were missing.

Another reason we distribute our group supplies is because we need to use our personal belongings to protect them. For example, wrapping crayons for 100 children for VBS in our personal t-shirts does offer some protection and cushion (but watch the heat—melting would be disastrous). If we are taking a few dozen Rice Krispies treats for the team, I can ask a few teens to use their shirts as protection so they won't get crushed.

Here are some things to consider when packing for the team:

Remember ministry supplies. This may include all the materials needed to run a successful VBS. This may include building materials and tools that your group may need to bring collectively. Carefully think through and talk about what is needed for each day, asking the right questions of your hosts and ministry partners.

Remember snacks and toiletries. Snacks and some toiletries for common use can also be something to consider for group packing. In both domestic and overseas trips we have taken, there have been some locations where our group has been afforded our own accommodations. It may be a house or church. Since the kitchen and bathrooms are for our exclusive use, it has been easier and very cost effective to buy certain products for the group to use together.

For example, instead of each team member buying individual shampoos, having one or two team members buy a regular size shampoo is more cost effective. Of course, there are a variety of shampoos and shampoo combinations with conditioners. Since the mission trip is short term, we ask for some team compromises. This is the same for toothpaste. Snacks can also be more cost effective if purchased in bulk for the team.

Hence, for a team of 15, for example, we know we usually take snacks including Slim Jims, Granola Bars, Pop Tarts, and Rice Krispies treats. For toiletries, we take soap/body wash, toothpaste, and shampoo. We will delegate one of these items to each person. So, if you are assigned a food item, we ask that you bring two dozen or more of that item. If you are assigned a toiletry item, we ask that you bring a family size of that item. Typically, we think of portions available at any discount club like Sam's, BJ's, or Costco. Most teens and parents have found that assigning one group item per person is advantageous over buying multiple individual items. Again, this is not possible for every mission trip, but when possible, it seems to work well for teens and parents.

Remember medications and first aid. A good first-aid kit, which includes Tylenol, Advil, and medicine for stomach aches, constipation, and diarrhea, is a must. If flying, I make sure to also pack a small version of my first-aid kit in my carry-on luggage.

If flying, especially overseas, make sure to have your teens pack any personal prescription medication in their carry-on luggage. If you are flying domestically, you should do the same, but many times it is a little easier to get a prescription filled if you are still in the United States. Adult leaders should also be aware of what personal prescription medications each teen needs before the trip. Many wise churches have prescription information forms that parents can fill out for their kids—much like they would fill out for their kids to have medication at school—so that there are no questions about dosing and a physician's phone number is readily accessible. (If your church has liability insurance, they may require you to use such a form anyway.)

While traveling—especially overseas—it may be difficult to locate feminine hygiene products, or the particular types that females need. This is an important consideration and sometimes a female adult leader can be designated to take care of this for the women before the trip. Finally, one last medication to consider bringing is something for motion sickness. For some teens on their first mission trip, a long van ride, an airplane trip, or a bus ride through rough terrain could get difficult.

Remember language/translation helps. When traveling outside the United States in particular, you need to think about communication on the mission field. I personally like to leave nothing to chance. If possible, I find a translator to join us on our mission trip. Or, talk to your hosts and make sure there is someone who can serve as a translator. English is a widespread, global language. Many countries learn English as a second language from a young age. People in many—often surprising—different locations know some English. However, there is quite a difference between knowing some English and being an effective translator. So, just be warned. Some may say they speak English, but it may not be at a level that would help with translation issues. Finally, you may need more than one translator at your mission site. For example, if you have a team of 15 people and you are doing VBS for 100 children, you will need a few translators.

I think it is also important when going overseas to at least learn some basic phrases for conversation. Even just a few basic phrases can help, along with their correct pronunciation. Below is an example of what we used for our STM trip to Hungary, as well as our ministry to the nomadic ethnic group better known as Gypsies. This kind of chart works well for our team to learn some phrases.

Come this way	Erre gyere
stand up please	Aljfel
lift up your head	A fejedet emeld fel
bow your head	A fejedet hajzsd le
sorry	Bocsanat
Let's pray	Imádkozzunk
I love you	Szeretlek
I will pray for you	En imadkozok erted
Thank you	Koszonom
Good morning	jo reggelt
Good evening	Jo estet
Hi	Szia
Hello	Sziaszto
Thank you	Koszonom
Yes	Igen
No	Nem
What is your name?	Hogy hivnak
God is love	Isten szeretet
Jesus is my Lord	Jezus Urum

Remember special gifts for hosts and/or a church offering. As briefly mentioned when discussing budgets, consider who you may visit, who may host you, and if you are visiting certain ministries or churches on your STM trip. In these cases, preparing a small gift for those hosting you or financial offerings to a ministry or church could be appropriate. I know many teams makes team t-shirts for their STM trip. If you do, I have found taking extra ones and giving them to those you meet who you are connecting with or who are hosting your group, is often very well received. Likewise, if you are serving with certain people at your location, a team t-shirt is always valued by them.

When going to a mission location, whether domestic or overseas, I also like to consider the host ministry or missionary and what unique needs they may have. I may not be able to bring everything they need, but it does not hurt to ask. In our urban church partnership, our host church said they had a need for a printer. Missionaries overseas may have difficulty in getting some items—or the items may just be extremely expensive in their locations. I remember a missionary asking for a certain printer ink cartridge because he could not get them at his mission field location. For any STM trip, the visiting team has a great opportunity to bring things that our host ministries or missionaries may need for ministry or may even need personally.

When we went to Haiti in 2010 and 2011, we knew that the food supply would be limited. My brother, who loves eating, ate only Pop Tarts even after doing surgery on patients for 12 hours a day. When our team went, we learned that there were relief workers who would stay long after we left. We brought tons of extra snacks like granola bars, crackers, Rice Krispies treats, and especially those pre-packaged canned tuna fish in mayo with crackers, which they appreciated.

Before our second trip, we called the host organization and the host missionary. Outside of the construction, we asked if he had any other needs—personal or ministry related. The pastor told us they had an urgent need for tarps. Many rural churches were still without a building or roofs on their buildings. While it was last minute, I purchased a tarp for each team member to take, one in each team member's luggage. Since we brought over 15 tarps with us, the host pastor was able to give them to different churches to protect their congregations from the rain and provide shade in the heat. As you prepare to go on an STM trip, a little inquiry can go a long way to fulfill unique and special needs.

Finally, in embracing a long-term view of missions and trying to nurture partnerships with mission trip hosts and locations, it is fine to go the first year and ask the host missionaries, churches, or organizations to give you a "tour" of all their ministries. Let them know that you want to learn about their ministry and needs, so you can partner with them. You may not be able to bring everything to a mission location the first year, but if you are fostering a long-term relationship, like I suggest, then the first year can be a window into seeing what things are of need, to bring on future visits.

Remember the little miscellaneous items that make all the difference. There are some random but handy things that I always pack for the group:

Sewing kit. A small travel sewing kit can be helpful. A team member may lose a button from their shorts or have a small tear that needs to get fixed.

Eyeglasses repair kit. Since I wear glasses, this is something I carry with me anyway. For teens who wear glasses, there may be occasions where minor repairs are needed. Also, the small screwdriver that comes with the kit has been useful for many other things. It makes me feel like MacGyver. (If you don't know who that is, it's okay, and I am dating myself.)

Notecards/encouragement notes. During the last few days of our trips, team members write notes/encouragement messages to each other, as well as to anyone they have served with at their location. It also serves as a good distraction or activity for teens in their down time.

Alarm clock. With cell phones nowadays, this may not be as important—provided you have a charger to plug in your phone every night. On our trips, we do ask the youth not to bring their phones. Hence, a few leaders should keep track and coordinate time issues and be responsible for setting their alarms—whether actual alarm clocks or phones—and waking up the team.

TIPS FOR GROUP PACKING AND AIRLINE TRAVEL

If you are traveling by plane, spreading the group packing items out among your team might be a necessity. If this is the case, numbering the group's luggage and keeping a list of what group items you have put where might sound like a lot of work, but it is so helpful on the other end when you arrive at your location—not only if a bag gets lost but also if you need to assess and prepare for each day's work.

As I have mentioned before, if you are doing VBS for a few days and each day you need to take certain materials for crafts, you know which bag has exactly what in it and you can make it accessible. You won't have to go rummaging through every bag to find what you are looking for. This is a life-saving group travel hack.

Here is an example of the first page of our luggage packing list:

NAME	BAG#	TEAM/GROUP ITEMS
John	1	Tool Bag Rice Krispies Treats (1) Sampoo (10) Gift Bags
Caleb	2	(1) Rice Krispies Treats (3) Waters (4) Pony beads bags (5) Carry bags

Ae-Ji	3	Toothpaste Pop-tart - 48 pack (1) Skit bag with shirts (1) Bubble (2) Shirts (2) Crayons (10) Gift bags
Luke	4	(1) Beef jerky (1) Twister Frisbee (1) Air pump (2) Bubbles Shirts Mug Hole-puncher (2) Tweezers (2) Scissors Carry bags (6) Pens – 12 pack
Noah	5	Radio Pen box Crayons (1) Seed bead bag (2) Safety Pin bags
Matt	6	(1) Mugs (3) Carry bags (10) Gift bags

I've also mentioned previously how handy pre-printed address labels are when travelling. (Remember they're nothing fancy, just the typical address label sheets you put in the printer—chances are your church already has a box.) But I'll mention again how perfect they are for everyone's baggage tags. Print a set with your destination address for your journey there and another set with the church address for the journey home.

PREPARING A PERSONAL PACKING LIST: A FEW IDEAS
I am not going to give you a detailed personal packing list that you need to give to each participant on your trip. You can find general

lists anywhere online. Instead, let me offer you some particular advice on personal packing lists and ideas that may be of help, to incorporate and share with your team.

Good luggage. Your luggage needs to endure the rough nature of traveling. The stress of being put into a van, thrown out of van, and the rigor of checking it in and eventually retrieving it from a conveyor belt, if you are flying, can be tough. Depending on the type of STM trip you go on, team members may each need a good, sturdy (but larger) piece of luggage that can also carry non-personal and team items such as tools and VBS supplies. When flying, don't forget to find out about **baggage allowance and weight policies** for luggage for your airline. (Reminder: This can impact your budget if bags are overweight.)

One final tip about luggage that I know many mission teams do and that I alluded to in chapter six. Find a unique duct tape color that can distinguish your teams' luggage from everyone else's at the airport. Since it may be hard to find one unique color, use two or three colors of duct tape instead. Tape it around the handles or put a strip (or strips) on each piece of luggage to help distinguish it from others. If putting duct tape on brand new luggage is an issue, the tape can be used to form a loose tag on the handle in such a way that it sticks to itself and not the bag.

Shoes and extra shoes. While serving, having a good pair of sneakers is much better and more practical than open-toed footwear such as slip-ons, flip-flops, or sandals. Even if you are not doing construction or heavy work, sneakers offer more protection. Our team actually mandates wearing sneakers when working.

While it takes up extra room, I always ask our team members to pack an extra pair of shoes. Especially ones they do not mind throwing away at the end of the trip if needed. Again, depending on the type of STM trip or even considering variables such as weather, it is always nice to have an extra pair of sneakers. They can get wet due to a sudden rain storm. They can get very messy if you are painting. Likewise, dried paint from your shoes could rub off all over someone's house. There are many situations where having an extra pair of shoes will come in handy.

Dirty clothes bag(s). Especially with teenage boys, who can perspire a lot when on an STM trip, having a place to put dirty laundry is important. No one needs to buy a special laundry bag. The plastic bags you get at the supermarket are adequate. Be sure each person brings a few. It is also good to instruct youth to dry any wet clothes or towels before putting them into a dirty clothes bag and packing them away. Not only will parents appreciate it (and I do as a parent), but if wet laundry is put into a dirty clothes bag early in a trip, it could mold or smell worse as the days go by. *Dry your dirty clothes first!* And bring those dirty clothes plastic bags.

Good backpack. Having a good, solid backpack comes in handy. For some types of trips your youth won't need to bring it around with them every day. But for other trips, it can be helpful for the team. Backpacks can carry the needs for the day like water, sunblock, snacks, and any work materials. They can help if you need to distribute VBS materials such as crafts to each teen. When flying, I ask each person to bring a backpack. Inside, they pack an extra change of clothes, any prescription medications, contact lenses, and some snacks, in case their luggage doesn't arrive on time or a missed/delayed connection leaves us stranded in an airport or hotel overnight without our luggage.

The non-negotiables. In the spirit of the "backpack of necessities" suggestion, here are some personal items that teens sometimes forget but really need:

- Personal medications, which need to be packed in a carry-on if flying (i.e., the backpack)
- Personal contact lenses and solution as well as extra glasses
- Toothbrushes (I always take a few extra)
- Underwear

You can make do with a lot of forgotten things on a trip, but these are really the ones that—if forgotten—will almost always have to be replaced.

Appropriate clothes. Find out if there will be any special events or perhaps churches/worship services you will be attending and the dress code for these events before you go on your STM trip. I know some people have suggested to always dress one level higher than the expectation. With teenagers, there is usually some forgiveness to this rule. Knowing what is culturally appropriate is important, particularly in predominantly Muslim countries. In any US church context, having teenagers show up in gym shorts, slippers, and t-shirts may be understandable to some, but I think it looks awful. When traveling overseas or visiting a church, I encourage teens to wear a pair of long khakis, a collared short-sleeved shirt (at the very least), and closed-toed shoes like sneakers. I also suggest belts, especially for guys.

Other times, you may be in a certain context where over-dressing could make your hosts uncomfortable, putting a socio-economic barrier you and those you are trying to serve. Try to be aware of how your clothing can fit in appropriately with respect to that unique culture and inform your group well in advance about these expectations. We all know teens who might need to borrow or buy what they would need for certain trips.

Overall, appropriate dress on a mission field may be different for each country. I was amazed that in many countries, wearing short pants in public is not the cultural norm. It is seen as something reserved for personal, home attire only. Likewise, when a bunch of "foreigners" are prancing around in shorts, it distinguishes them in ways that can be a stumbling block for those we meet in the mission field.

We also want to encourage modest dress on the mission field. For girls, this means that shirts with spaghetti straps are not appropriate in my group. We ask all our youth to wear modest t-shirts as well—guys and girls. In general, we as a team just want to make sure our clothes are not inappropriate and are not offensive or distracting.

We also want to be sensitive not only to those we are coming to serve but also to our fellow teammates. In group bunking situations where we have shared showers and bathrooms, it is important to be mindful of what we're wearing. We have been on trips in years past when it had to be announced that males had to wear shirts and shorts to the bathroom, because they were just going in boxers, practically naked. Some young females were just wearing towels wrapped around them. Even when it's just our own group at a location, these little details have to be discussed, so we can be modest.

Shower slippers. Unless you are staying in a home, bathroom and shower accommodations on many STM trips will likely be some sort of public bathroom space and shower facility that will be shared with others. In my experience, it's a gym shower or showers in a dormitory of some kind. Whatever it is, these are—it bears repeating—*public* facilities *shared* with others, whether just the people in your group or complete strangers. In these cases, I strongly suggest teens wear shower slippers. It is not so much a paranoia or fear but just a safer option than bare feet. One note is that the shower slippers should be plastic or quick-drying. Be wary of sports slippers that have cloth material of some kind, which don't dry quickly and stay wet for quite a while.

Nalgene bottle. Continually buying bottled water is expensive on any trip. Hence, having each member of your team bring a Nalgene-type water bottle will not only save money but also will be more convenient. On domestic trips, it is usually fairly easy to find water fountains for teens to fill up their bottles. On international trips, you may not always be able to drink tap water. Rather, people in certain countries purchase large tanks of bottled water. Hence having Nalgene bottles is a must.

Though Nalgene bottles say "germ/bacteria free," after five to seven days, they do smell and can get nasty. At least every five days on longer trips, a few volunteers collect and wash all our bottles. It's more sanitary, particularly if any flu or cold hits your group.

Another tip is that on trips where you are flying, you can fill up your bottles *after* you go through the TSA security line. We all know how expensive any type of drink is at the airport. Hence, having your group carry *empty* bottles with their backpacks and then fill them with water after going through TSA security line is a good way to save money.

Bible, pen, and journal. As I've already said, my preference is that our group not bring electronics on trips. Your group may be different and that's great. Either way, I make sure each person brings a Bible, at least one pen to write things down, and some sort of journal. (*Mission Tripping: An Interactive Journal* was created for teens with this journal space in mind and contains plenty of space for them to write their thoughts and reflections, should you chose to utilize it.) I have found that having our youth journal each evening and morning during the mission trip (and at group meeting times) is a great exercise and useful for each individual. You might even ask volunteers to share their thoughts and reflections from their journals periodically.

A light jacket. A light jacket will often be helpful, particularly if weather is unpredictable or if you are flying—some teens are sensitive to temperature changes and some flights can get chilly.

Sleeping needs. This really varies from trip to trip, location to location, and between domestic trips and going overseas. Make sure you ask the right questions and know if you are going to need sleeping bags, pillows, or even air mattresses. It impacts the packing for each person and the team significantly if you need to supply even so much as your own sheets.

A flashlight. You may need them at many locations. Your group may need them even for something as simple as going to the bathroom at night. Be sure to find out whether or not these are needed for your mission trip location.

Sunscreen/sunglasses. These days, more people are aware of the need for protection from the sun. Hence, depending on whether or not your work will be outside, sunglasses and sunscreen might be things that are easily forgotten but much needed.

CHAPTER 9 | PREPARING THE CHURCH/ PARENTS

Over the years, I have introduced the STM trip program for the youth group at our church and have also introduced many new locations for STM trips. In this chapter, I offer some practical advice for proposing and preparing your church/parents for youth STM trips. Working *with* church leadership, church mission departments, and parents through the various aspects of an STM trip is an important part of planning and going, as well as returning.

COMMUNICATE WITH YOUR CHURCH

It is extremely helpful to plan early for your STM trips. It shows ownership, and as a youth worker, you can better shape the vision and purpose for the trip. I like to communicate with my senior pastor, church leadership, and mission board 18 months prior to any potential STM trips. *Please know*, if you're reading this book in the fall (10 months or so before next summer) or even the spring (a few months before the approaching summer) do not panic. You can still pull off a great STM trip. I have done it that way quite a few times. Of course, if you want to go with a missions organization, it may be tough to find a location for your group on short notice.

In communicating early (and often) with your church leadership, you typically have more control and can influence the agenda of the trip. You can prepare and present the budget you may need to the church. Your church leadership will know how much you will be asking each of your youth and families to pay or fundraise. You can begin to convey the purpose and rationale for taking teens on a particular STM trip. You can begin to pray and have others join you in prayer. You can begin thinking about the calendar and schedule of the church and youth and when would be the best time for your mission trip.

Your church may manage events and programs based on the calendar. We've talked about considering the local school calendars when planning dates for an STM trip, because summer break is the most obvious time to take youth on an STM trip. But you also have to consider the church schedule as well and how the youth play into it. For example, our church does VBS in late June. We also like to take a mission trip in late June. Since many of the youth group teens serve the VBS ministry, we try to consider the different schedules within our church, not negatively impacting another ministry with our absence, if possible. If you want to plan a commissioning service or mission report for after your return, it's vital to identify an open date for either of these early as well. As a church youth ministry, you are promoting your mission trip not just as a youth group trip but a trip that the entire church has championed. Another effective way this is done is through prayer and the prayer ministry, so that the whole church can support your youth group STM trips.

COMMUNICATE WITH THE PARENTS

There are a few vital things that can and need to be communicated with the parents of the teenagers going on the trip. I have done these things chronologically, from when we first begin to prepare for a mission trip through when we return.

Offer a mission trip information meeting/orientation. Inviting parents to a meeting to orient them to your youth group STM trip is vital. Parents will have important questions. Sending their teenager away for any extended period of time can be terrifying for some. They will need details of dates and responsibilities that their teenagers will have. One way we try to curb any barrage of questions is by mailing STM trip information before the orientation with parents. They receive the dates, trip details, and costs in writing. At the meeting, we talk about fundraising to alleviate costs of the trips. I also communicate to parents that mission trip fees and costs are non-refundable after committing to a trip. There is a "commitment by" date, when an initial deposit is due to reserve a participant's spot. For overseas trips, there is also a time (very early) when we need to buy airline tickets. We can have parents get airline credit back if they cancel, but airlines do not refund money after a ticket is purchased.

Communicate STM trip youth meeting information and covenants. With the busyness in the lives of teenagers and their parents, I have found it very important to communicate the mission team meeting schedule and have an accountability process for attendance at every meeting. As I noted earlier, an effective STM trip is somewhat curriculum or discipleship based, or at the very least, it's dependent on preparation. Even if less mature believers are going, both youth and parents need to know the commitment involved. This is not just some one-day event or social justice trip.

In my youth group, we communicate the entire mission team meeting schedule with parents. In addition, we make it clear that they can miss up to two meetings. After missing two meetings, we contact the parents and teen and set up a meeting with them to communicate that the youth is at risk of not being able to go on the trip. Believe me, these have been some of the most difficult meetings to have. Especially if parents have paid an initial deposit for the trip out of their own pockets. But if this meeting schedule and expectations for attendance are communicated early, you will not face such issues. While I want as many of our youth to experience STM trips as possible, there have been times that I "suggested" parents not send their teen if attendance at meetings was going to be an issue.

Stay in communication while in process. I have heard from teachers in local middle schools and high schools that it is hard to get parents to read emails and flyers that are sent home. In fact, I am probably a case study for that, because as a parent of teenagers, I do not read most of the flyers sent home or emails from school. But packing lists and certain supplies are a must for an STM trip. Because just sending STM trip information home with teenagers may not always mean the parents receive it, let alone read it, we have thought about two ways to solve this.

First, you can have a "mid-preparation" meeting for parents during the weeks leading up to the STM trip. (A month or so before you leave is also a good time.) Whatever you choose, this is where you reiterate important details of your packing list. (Just know that no matter what you send home or how many meetings you have, there will always be those who do things at the last minute.) This meeting can also serve as a Q&A time for parents. Finally, this meeting can be a great time to pray with parents for the mission trip and their teenagers.

Second, when I do send a packing list home with teens, I send two lists. I ask one to be sent back to me, signed by both the parent and the teen. Honestly, I don't know if parents even read these before signing, but at least it offers a level of accountability.

For trips where we fly, I've explained already that we gather at church a few days before we leave and pack our luggage and (especially) make sure they meet the weight requirements. This is to alleviate surprises at the airport and avoid paying overweight baggage fees. Once in a while, a parent complains about having to bring their teenager's luggage early. One year, a parent said they were not informed of this, when their child did not come with their luggage ready to be packed and weighed. The parent got rather indignant. That was, until we showed them the packing list they had signed and the date for packing the teen's luggage.

Meet with parents again right before the trip. A few days before the trip or even the day of the trip, I gather parents. We give them detailed information about our return, a daily agenda of what we will be doing (so they can pray for us), reminders of contact information (as well as reminders of the limited availability of Wi-Fi if we are going to some remote domestic or overseas location), and we spend time in prayer. I particularly like that giving parents a detailed agenda of what we will be doing each day of our trip has alleviated any curiosity about or fear as to what their teenagers may be doing during their STM trip. Here you will see a sample trip agenda and calendar

Sunday	Monday	Tuesday	Wednesday	Thursday	Friday	Saturday
June 17 Leave for ___	18	19 Arrive	20 Bus leaves 8:00 a.m. Orphanage Trip (Cleaning, caring for children and Korean Dance) Counseling Classes	21 10:00 a.m. – 3:00 p.m. Village Trip Children's ministry & Labor (2 Team split) Counseling Classes	22 10:00 a.m. – 3:00 p.m. Village Trip Children's ministry & Labor (2 Team split) Counseling Classes	23 Fellowship & Games with the Village
24 Worship at Local Church	25 9:30 a.m. – 4:30 p.m. (Bus leaves 8:00 a.m.) Rise & Shine Youth Conference	26 9:30 a.m. – 4:30 p.m. (Bus leaves 8:00 a.m.) Rise & Shine Youth Conference	27 9:30 a.m. – 4:30 p.m. (Bus leaves 8:00 a.m.) Rise & Shine Youth Conference	28 9:30 a.m. – 4:30 p.m. (Bus leaves 8:00 a.m.) Rise & Shine Youth Conference	29 Overnight Outdoor Trip to National Park	30 City Tour and Souvenirs
July 1 Leave for US						

we give to our parents. (This is from an actual overseas trip in 2012. The location is a place where things are still sensitive for Christians, so I deleted the name of the country.)

An important note about parents who want to accompany their teenagers on an STM trip: I am a believer in STM trips and intergenerational ministry in general. I have read much and have also written about the impact that intergenerational mission trips can have. In my personal doctoral research on innovation in the context of churches and youth ministry, I have also found that things like intergenerational mission trips have a great impact on youth, especially their long-term faith commitments after they age out of youth group.

However, I do think it's important to cautiously consider the particular cases where parents want to go on the same mission trip as their own teenagers. In this era of helicopter and hovering parents, I have had to screen parents to make sure they are not going just to "protect" their own children unnecessarily or going with any other particular agenda. In recent years, our church has offered one distinct mission trip as a vehicle for families who want to go together. In the end, however, there is the need for both intergenerational mission trips and STM trips just for youth with other adult leaders.

If a parent does want to go with his child, I usually ask the teen how he feels about the parent coming. I also talk to the parent about it. If there is disagreement about whether a parent should or should not volunteer for the teenager's mission trip, I tell the parent they can volunteer for a different trip. It is at that moment where it is easy to see if the parent "really" wanted to go on a mission trip or just *his* teenager's mission trip.

CHAPTER 10 | PREPARING THE TEAM:
(YOUTH AND ADULT LEADERS)

My wife and I still actively watch the CBS show *Survivor*. One of the interesting aspects of the show is thrusting the new competitors into a different environment each season. Some adjust very well and some not so well. The mental demands of being in an unfamiliar environment are one thing. But even the physical demands with heat, fatigue, and hunger take a huge toll on some of the competitors, sometimes early on during the 39-day adventure. It's always amazing to me to see competitors who are so ill-prepared for the show, especially when one million dollars is at stake.

TRAINING RIGHT

I am not going to say that an STM trip is far more precious than one million dollars, so much more is at stake. But I will say that I am just as aghast seeing STM team participants who clearly did not train for their service. I hope this chapter emphasizes that whether going on a show like *Survivor* or an STM trip, participants must prepare—in many different ways.

I have read numerous books about STM trips, and there are tons of factors related to going on them. It's hard to comprehend them all. However, I will say that in my experience working with teenagers, these are the most valuable ways to prepare them:

Have mandatory preparation meetings. An important part of the overall preparation for the STM trip is to provide the youth with a clear and mandatory meeting schedule, including the post-STM trip meetings. I understand that the lives of teenagers include sports demands, academic demands, social demands, and family obligations. However, I believe it is important for youth (and parents) to know the importance of STMs and missions in general. My teenage boys have played (and are still playing) sports in middle school and high school. I have never seen a coach let them miss practices and then just show up and play in a game. Never! The same is true with a school play or academic club. I realize there are always exceptions, and teenagers *will* have conflicts in their schedules. But STMs are also a huge and important endeavor, and preparation meetings need to be communicated to the youth and parents through a clear meeting schedule.

In our youth group, we allow teens to miss up to two meetings. We understand that things come up. In light of this, after teens register for missions, we give them a few initial meetings to decide if they will be able to attend meetings and fully prepare for the STM trip, before their deposits are due and full commitment is required.

Be purposeful about spiritual discipleship. As discussed earlier in the book, the intersection of discipleship and missions is what I am thinking about as I prepare youth spiritually for missions trips. I hope that through the STM experience, they can grow in their faith, even those less spiritually mature. I firmly believe that an STM trip is both a mission and a way to walk with Jesus. Spiritual growth can be nurtured through an STM trip. For example, a teen's view of loving others, compassion, justice, mercy, and obviously missions itself, can all be nurtured and grown through the trip.

Hence, elements of spiritual preparation for an STM trip must include teaching theological aspects of ecclesiology and missions, which incorporate a short-term but also a long-term component. They need to be continually reminded that missions is both "short term" and long term as a lifestyle and practice. Spiritual preparation, as well as the idea of missions as the overall umbrella of the STM trip, must be part of the youth ministry before and long after the trip. Missions and service must be incorporated as a major foundation of the youth group year round and as part of its core teachings throughout the year.

In Section V of this book, you'll be able to see this preparation in more practical terms. It contains the Leader's Guide for *Mission Tripping: An Interactive Journal*, which is essentially a blueprint for discipleship through 15 team meetings and times of personal reflection/prayer. It incorporates material important for the upcoming STM trip and also material that allows participants to be molded with a long-term view of missions. My prayer is that the Interactive Journal (and the leader's guide) will be helpful and act as a curriculum to prepare your youth and help them participate more diligently. (See page 205.)

Set clear expectations of physical demands. I once had a youth intern implement physical training as part of each mission preparation meeting before we went to serve in the rural mountain areas of northern Kenya. I was amused and happy to see the youth sweat, get a good workout, and even complain as we would "march" around the church to get physically ready for the trip. Moreover, it actually *was* beneficial, because when we got to the northern area of Kenya, the experience was very rigorous on our bodies.

While I am not saying you should do a workout together, I think elements of physical preparation must be considered and discussed at mission meetings. At minimum, you should talk about the conditions you expect to live and function in on the trip and prepare participants to for those realities. For example:

> **Weather.** What the weather will be like and how it will affect your mission trip is important to discuss. We had one teen who loved to play basketball. After serving all day at our mission work site, he would play basketball for hours during the evening, because the place where our team was staying had a court. After two days of this, he wound up cramping up during our evening devotional time and being exhausted during the day when we were doing our work. We eventually had to ask him not to play basketball for a few days. He was not aware of how much the weather was

impacting him.

Keeping hydrated in the heat should be discussed. In my trips to Haiti, we were warned to drink at least eight 32 oz. Nalgene bottles of water a day, and we were still on the verge of dehydration (which you can tell by having very little urine or a bright yellow urine color). Overall, the weather and its impact on each person is a valuable matter to discuss before going on an STM trip.

Outdoor living. This may sound a little stereotypical, but we know that children and teenagers do not play outside as much as they should or did in prior generations. They have become couch potatoes, indoor creatures, and fixated on electronics. While teenagers are also resilient, the "shock" of being outdoors or in a non-air-conditioned environment in the summer is quite an adjustment for many. Truthfully, I'm not sure what you or I can do about this as team leaders before such a trip. (Perhaps taking them to a sauna and having them sit there without their cell phones?) Whatever it may be, I do want to prepare our youth—at least mentally—for the work and walking they will do outdoors.

Sleep schedule. Since many are beginning or on summer break before your STM trip, their sleep schedules may be affected or reversed from their normal school year. I know in the summer, many teenagers turn into night owls. It is important to address the sleep schedule on the STM trip, the need for rest at night, and the need to have energy for each day. I can remember a few years back a teen was in the habit of playing video games all night, right up until the day of the trip. When we left for the mission trip, the first four days were a battle just to try to get him adjusted to "daytime" living. It was quite a chore for him. Ultimately, I think it is of value to prepare certain teens to have a "normal" sleep schedule.

Prepare your youth for eating far from home. There are two important things youth need to know about food. First, the need for actual physical nourishment (not just junk) is very real—a need often neglected by teens. It is something some of them don't think much about. Adults and teenagers alike need food for energy. However, even on a domestic mission trip, meals are different than eating foods from the comforts of your home, grabbing a pizza or fast food, or having your parents make your food. Even something simple like waking up for breakfast in the summer can be a shock for some. We may be eating from a cafeteria morning and night. We may get fatigued and not *want* to eat. While I do not want to *force* teens to eat, I remind them of the need for physical nourishment.

Second, sometimes we may be offered food we are not used to. Going overseas, we know that the food will be different. However, being culturally sensitive to unique foods that our teenagers will be introduced to is also something we need to talk about. On our first trip to Africa, the locals from the remote mountain prepared a huge feast for us. It was roasted goat meat. My youth had never tasted goat. Since these goats were more free-range as well, the meat tasted particularly gamey. I am not sure how one describes gamey meat to a person who's never had it, but it is uniquely different than the meat most teens eat at home. I think it's just something one has to taste to understand. It's just very, very distinctive. And frankly, this meat was hard for them to eat.

Likewise, even on domestic trips, a person or individual family may prepare dinner for our team. Even a home-cooked meal may seem unusual or strange when it's not your family's cooking. On our mission trip to Philadelphia each year, we are surrounded by various ethnic communities. For some teens, eating foods from a different ethnic community can be difficult.

Before we leave on any STM trip, whether domestic or foreign, we try to prepare youth for these unique eating situations. We instruct them on simple things like being polite, trying to eat what they are given/offered, not reacting to a taste in a loud manner that makes them stand out, and smiling with a thankful disposition throughout the meal. Of course in many cases, nothing will be like what you'll eat on the trip, but if possible, try some of what will be the local fare in advance. The internet has many international recipes if no food from that culture is readily available in your area.

As you're about to read, I am also going to suggest watching some shows of celebrity chef Anthony Bourdain. He is an adventurous eater, but even for him, some things are too much. However, how he responds to the hosts who serve him foods that are hard to eat is a model for any short-term missionary.

Set clear expectations of the (cross-)cultural elements. Whether it be an STM trip to an urban context, a rural area, or overseas, almost every STM has some sort of cross-cultural element. Youth will be encountering new customs, people, and ways of doing things.

For example, when buying souvenirs overseas, especially in local markets, many countries accept the practice of haggling for items, which is negotiating a fair price. However, when you tell teenagers this, sometimes they can become rude in attempting to do it themselves. It's culturally unfamiliar for them. This is where the "ugly American" can rear its head. (This is a great thing to ask the local missionary about in advance.) Teenagers may simply need a reminder to be fair. They need to remember that the other person is trying to make a living, not playing a game. Knowing how to haggle politely— without being rude or insulting—is a cultural issue, and it's just one of many you can encounter when taking teenagers on an STM trip before you even get to the cultural aspects of ministry there.

I have used *Ministering Cross-Culturally: An Incarnational Model for Personal Relationship* by Sherwood G. Lingenfelter and Marvin K. Mayers, in various seminary classes over the years, to teach about doing ministry in different cross-cultural contexts.[1] It is an excellent book, discussing how elements such as time, dealing with crisis, authenticity, goals, and self-worth are viewed differently from other cultural perspectives. I highly suggest this book for adults, and it can be used to highlight some aspects of cultural awareness for teens as well. In fact, you can use it as a discussion piece for your youth if you see fit, to prepare them for new encounters with different people they may meet on their STM trips.

However, teenagers are not seminary or graduate-level students. They sometimes need communication that is intellectually more accessible. For my group, I like to show them clips of well-known celebrity chef Anthony Bourdain. He may not be a Christian (at least as far as I know), but he is probably the best model of a "cross-cultural missionary" I have ever seen. I mean that. For example, in an interview with Piers Morgan in 2012 that you can show your group, I love the way he talks about the "most disgusting" thing he has ever eaten.[2] But more importantly, he discusses issues related to cultural sensitivity when eating foods from other cultures. This is a fantastic interview to share with your teens.

Also, try to find a copy of one of my favorite episodes of his television show *Anthony Bourdain: No Reservations.* In season three, episode four, his trip to Namibia contains a great example of cross-cultural sensitivity.[3] I have never had so much respect for someone in a difficult cross-cultural situation. After the Namibian tribesmen caught and cooked a warthog, they offered the anus, filled with warthog "poo," to Bourdain. His desire to be culturally sensitive and aware of the Namibian tribesmen and their dignity is a great example of caring and embracing the culture of others. Along with these clips, rather than using academics or theory with youth, I have found that three simple things have worked in guiding them to a humble but profound cross-cultural heart that prepares them for new and different encounters.

Openness. Since many of our teenagers may be traveling outside their local area for the first time, I try to cultivate a sense of openness. I use the word *openness* as a way of conveying to them the need to be open to new ideas, new ways of doing things, and new foods. They do not necessarily have to adopt and embrace everything they encounter. But I teach them to at least be open to them.

Humility. It takes humility to be open. I know most teenagers are not necessarily prideful, per se. But it takes humility to be open. I like the simple definition that Merriam-Webster uses, defining humility as "the quality or state of not thinking you are better than other people: the quality or state of being humble."[4] Teenagers may unknowingly act like they are better than others. But I think that speaks more of their developmental stage of life than their hearts. When taught well, they can also be very humble and generous to others.

Teachability. With openness and humility, youth can also be *learners.* I try to promote this posture for our teens. Long after the STM trip, in our globalized world, they will encounter new things. They are, in fact, probably learning new things every day. In helping them understand and value learning and being teachable, we are preparing them to open themselves to new things, to seek to understand, and to be able to at least accept differences.

After introducing them to being open, humble, and teachable, I also introduce them to the Apostle Paul. He is often considered one of the great or greatest missionaries in the Bible. A good passage from the Apostle Paul to expound upon and one that will help your youth be even more aware of being open, humble, and teachable is 1 Corinthians 9:19-23. Paul's heart to be "contextual" to those he will be ministering to teaches us a great deal about ministry in different contexts and to different cultures. From this passage, I have teens explore the idea of being open, humble, and teachable and have them further think about these concepts as "missionaries."

Communicate clear fundraising information and goals. All STM team members in most churches and youth groups have to pay for their trip somehow. Early on, it is very important to tell teens how your team will do this and the requirements for each teen. In the last chapter, I discussed the need to talk with parents about fundraising. However, the youth need to comprehend these expectations as well, in conjunction with their parents. I think fundraising will reflect the teens' hearts and motives for their STM trip. (In other words, if they are not working to raise funds for a mission trip, perhaps they have rich parents and are spoiled? It happens.) In general, individual fundraising *can* be effective. However, if teens have parents or relatives to support them, it may be much easier for them to raise funds for their STM trip than others who may have unsupportive non-Christian families or families that simply cannot realistically contribute much. Thus, I make sure to promote a *team* or *corporate* strategy for fundraising, so that everyone will be involved in the process. Ultimately, just be clear on how you will do fundraising, individually or corporately. Moreover, if it is more of a team or corporate structure, be sure to plan specific fundraisers as a team.

Provide practical training for ministry tasks. Each mission field, domestic and overseas, will have certain ministry task that are specific to that context. Likewise, you may have a personal desire to do a certain type of ministry. In working with missions organizations, you may be able to find an organization that can fit your ministry desires. In chapter two, I talked about trying to focus on more "systemic" solutions for STM trips.

In our first year going to Haiti, I wanted our team to help rebuild places where buildings and other structures were destroyed. Even just finding places to help clean up and remove the destruction was my hope. However, before we got there, I learned from the initial responders and Haitian pastors that trying to do any rebuilding projects could be dangerous. Many buildings were still not stable or safe for us to go into. There were also many Haitians still fearful for their lives and worried that another earthquake could happen. Similarly, being a nation that practiced voodoo for a long time, many felt frightened and cursed after the earthquake. Some Haitians were just afraid of being indoors in case another earthquake hit. Our team learned that this was part of the reason why so many stayed in tents and tent villages.

I am glad I asked about the needs that were present in Haiti the first few months after the earthquake and before we left. I really wanted to do construction work that first year, but there were other ministry needs.

Two important things about serving can be learned from this:

Listen carefully to the ministry leaders of the mission trip

location you are going to *prior* to going. Talk to local people and ministries, if at all possible. Ask your host organizations or missionaries about the actual needs. They will know a lot more about what you can prepare for, ministry-wise. If you are asked to do VBS, you will be better prepared for it with culturally appropriate and creative crafts, songs, and games. If you are called to do evangelism, you can prepare ways to share the gospel through things like small skits, outreach activities, and conversations with non-Christians—all of which need to be practiced prior to going. If you are called to do some sort of construction, repairs, or manual labor, you can prepare tools and materials as needed beforehand and perhaps get a little training from professionals in your church too. Overall, it is the leader's job to know and prepare the youth properly for their ministry tasks. Hence, being as aware as possible beforehand will make both your training and service more fruitful.

When you arrive on the mission field, ask your hosts if they can show you the different ministries they are already doing. While working with a church in our local major city and hearing about their existing ministry, we came to learn their hope of having a computer learning center one day. In subsequent years, we worked with the ministry to secure laptops and computer programs to help start their initiative. By just asking the hosts to show you around, you can learn how to serve alongside them both on that trip and in the future, building a long-term relationship for your STM trips.

Provide clear packing lists, including what *not* to bring. Clearly, packing lists are a must, as previously discussed. But it can be just as important to address the issue of what *not* to bring on an STM trip. There are two things I have in mind, but you will have to decide what is best for your group.

First, academic/summer school work can be an issue. This may not be a problem in many youth groups, but it can be. I have seen students bring SAT study materials and summer reading on STM trips. Understand, I am all for academic efforts. But at times, they can become a distraction and teens can set themselves apart from the group. I let our teens bring one summer reading book as well as some study material for the van or plane rides to and from a location. However, during the trip, I ask them to put these things aside. Believe me, once they get in a van with their friends, they usually forget about their work anyway. If you are going on a longer plane ride, especially overseas, teens will probably want to watch the movies on the plane. However, it has been a good practice to let our youth know our expectations regarding school work.

Electronics such as cell phones, digital cameras, and iPods are the second area where you will have to come up with your own policies for your group. On any mission trip, the biggest concern I have is teens losing these expensive gadgets or even theft. Especially with the costs of these things and the cost to replace them. It is never easy for a parent to find out their teenager lost an expensive phone or broke a nice digital camera.

I understand the value of electronics and have addressed them in the following way. For pictures, I have one or two teens bring cameras and take pictures for the whole group. There are all sorts of reasons why youth want to bring their cell phones, and picture taking is one of them. But we know if they bring them and use them, it can also become a distraction. Moreover, parents often want our youth to have them, especially to contact them. For parents, I provide *my* cell phone number and let them know they can call me. Likewise, if a young person *really* needs to call their parents, I let them call on my phone.

In recent years, we have found a compromise or balance to this on domestic trips, which you may think is crazy. We collect phones and hold on to them. On our leisure days, I let our youth have them. They can listen to music, take pictures, or go online. In overseas locations, I have not done this, partly because of the ridiculous roaming charges they may incur.

For domestic trips, I have found holding the phones to be a good balance. It keeps teens from being distracted during the trip but gives them some leeway to take pictures, update Facebook, and call parents if needed. I used to be one of those people who would not permit phones at all. However, this compromise has worked well for the sake of our domestic trips and the desires of both the youth and their parents.

One other issue to think about with cell phones and electronics is charging them when on a trip. It may not sound like a big deal, but finding outlets for a group of phones may be tricky. I always pack a power strip or two, even if only our leaders are bringing phones. In addition, if you go overseas, you may need adapters for different electric outlets and voltages.

Ultimately, there is no right or wrong answer to this issue. My various youth worker friends all have their own viewpoints and ways they go about their policies on this issue. I respect them all, and you will just need to find out what works best for your group.

Give guidance about keeping in touch with those you meet. In my early years of STM trips, and especially working with missionaries overseas, our visiting teams were often warned not to give out personal information to people we met. This was for the safety of our youth. Back then, in the early '90s, I would have teens give out our church address and church phone number if anyone asked to correspond with our team members.

But in this electronically connected world today, it seems even in some of the more remote locations we travel to for missions, most people have access to email and Facebook. I want to love and trust the people we encounter in our mission work, but I am also protective of our teenagers. We have had a few times when people we have met have solicited our teens for money after the trip. As STM teams, we also do not want to be rude or offensive to the people we meet in the mission field by giving no information. So, if there is any question or worry, I tell our teens that I will ask the local ministry leaders or missionaries first—that's when the church number and address come in handy.

In recent years, especially when our teenagers meet other teenagers, they all seem so connected electronically that I usually let them become Facebook friends with an understanding that if anything suspicious occurs, they will let me know. Clear guidelines in this regard are worth noting to your youth as you prepare them—as well as how to communicate their answer to those who ask for contact information.

REGARDING ADULT LEADERS

As far as adult leaders and their preparation, I noted them in the title of this chapter because I believe it is vital that they participate in the preparation and training with the youth in order to—if nothing else—know what is expected of them and the youth. That said, there may be a few guidelines that don't apply to them but still impact them. For example, I understand that as adults they may need their cell phones daily on a mission trip. Knowing that on our trips kids have limited (or no) access to their phones, I ask them to be discreet in their use of them.

I also always want our adults to be good role models. Hence, as far as something like cultural sensitivity, they need to understand they may be encountering new things just like the teenagers. In that way, their willingness to prepare diligently and lead by example in the moment can provide direction and guidance for teens in new situations.

Ultimately, if the adults are adult *leaders,* then it is important that they don't just show up the day of the trip. That lack of preparation and engagement could have a devastating impact on your team. Rather, adult leaders should be fully part of the mission team, which hopefully means modeling and leading their teenagers at every turn of the trip, from the preparation meetings through your mission and beyond.

CHAPTER 11 | PREPARING MINDS & HEARTS: ON MISSION, NOT VACATION

There is one last area of pre-trip preparation for your group that we can't overlook. For years, to help youth (and leaders) focus on what an STM trip is all about, I've been using a table, included in this chapter, to illustrate the major differences between a vacation and a mission trip. It is important to focus on these differences, especially knowing the critique that STM trips can be too touristy. Likewise, because teenagers are often going to be "teenagers" (goofy, wanting to have fun, and sometimes not focused), it is important to highlight the differences between a vacation and a mission trip.

BREAKING IT DOWN

The table on the next page is a visual outline that helps communicate this philosophy of "mission not vacation" to the youth. (The Interactive Journal contains a "fill in the blank" exercise for this table—which you can see in Section V, on page 216.) Here are the details you and your youth may need to understand what is meant by each of the points on the table:

1. Serve Self vs. Serve Others. I love vacations. I probably love them even more because I rarely take them. But even in my daily life, I do make sure to treat myself to an hour or two of pure leisure. It may not sound thrilling or exotic, but I try to watch a few hours of television at the end of each night. Moreover, this usually is time for my wife and I to be alone when our children (now teenagers) are asleep. It is pure enjoyment and it is purely for myself. Vacations and leisure

VACATION	MISSION TRIP
1. Serve Self	1. Serve Others
2. Inward Focus	2. Outward Focus
3. Paying to Have Fun (Although you will have fun)	3. Paying (Fundraising) to Work Hard
4. Paying to Be Served	4. Fundraising to Serve
5. The Cost of Enjoying Self	5. The Cost of Sacrifice
6. Fee Shows You Want to Go	6. Dedication Shows You Want to Go
7. Fee Reserves Your Spot	7. Dedication and Commitment Confirm/Affirm Your Spot
8. Little or No Work	8. Hard Work, Homework, Heart Work
9. Fun for Me	9. Heart of Me
10. Unity = Togetherness	10. Unity = United with/in Christ & His Purpose
11. No Cares About Life	11. Cares About Life in Christ and Others
12. No Cares About Our Actions	12. Words and Action Either Display Christ or the Opposite
13. Once a Summer	13. Long Before and After the Summer

are time for ourselves. On every STM trip, we do find time for some personal rest and even relaxation and some souvenir shopping time. I am all for that. However, I make sure to tell our teenagers that our first and foremost reason for these trips is to serve others. The focus *needs* to be on serving others.

2. Inward Focus vs. Outward Focus. Perhaps overlapping with the prior point, it is fine while on a vacation to be focused only on yourself, focused inwardly. It's fine to only worry about one's own enjoyment and pleasure, what one is going to eat, how one is going to have fun that day, and how one may spend the day. However, on an STM trip, the focus must be outward. We are thinking about those we are serving. We also must think about the STM team, the people hosting us, and the folks we are going to serve (for example: *their* house, *their* church, *their* neighborhood). We know the stereotype that teenagers are focused on themselves and self-obsessed (but we love them). And STM trips are a great place/time for teens to begin thinking outwardly and more about others.

In particular, the team dynamics of your STM group should not be overlooked. I am sure that many of your teenagers may live with siblings. But spending an extended period of time with an STM team will make it evident that your youth group teens are not used to sharing space outside of family. A few examples are sharing a bathroom with a group, cleaning up after themselves for the sake of others, and how they eat and share food that is meant for a group. One year, three teens were hungry and asked if they could have a few Rice Krispies treats. They ate *three* boxes of them. These were not only for our team, we had planned to give them to some of the children we met. It was a great reminder that we need to prepare and help our teens to think *team* first and more generally, *others* first.

3. Paying to Have Fun (Although you *will* have fun) vs. Paying (Fundraising) to Work Hard. STM trips are going to cost money. That is a fact. We have to pay for them. But sometimes because we are paying for them, there can be a conscious or subconscious consumer mentality. Teenagers pay to go to the movies, pay to go on ski trips with their school ski clubs, and even pay to do certain fun youth group activities. Hence, we expect some kind of return or product for what we paid for. I try to make it clear to our group that on an STM trip, we are paying/fundraising to work hard. We are giving our money so we can go serve and to help others. Our expectation must not be something we get or gain, but rather what we can *give*. We are not consumers, purchasing something. We are paying to serve.

4. Paying to Be Served vs. Fundraising to Serve. Like the prior point, an STM trip is not like entering a restaurant and having a waiter or waitress come serve you. We are not paying for something tangible like food and are not paying tips so we can be served. We are raising funds and money to serve others. I often talk about the example of Jesus washing the disciples' feet in John 13. Jesus was performing an act that was reserved for servants. Servants were performing this act because it was their livelihood and it was what they were getting paid to do or told to do. Jesus, however, did it as an example of servanthood. There is a huge difference between being served and serving—something I want to remind our youth of in the preparation for our trip.

5. The Cost of Enjoying Yourself vs. The Cost of Sacrifice. I don't want to give the impression that mission trips cannot be fun. On our trips, we do schedule in a day of fun and relaxation. Moreover, we have fun in fellowship with each other, especially hanging out at night. Sometimes it seems like a huge lock-in every day. But while we can have fun, we did all the fundraising because we are servants of Christ. We are sacrificing our summer and our time in view of God's mercy to offer our lives to him, as Romans 12:1 says.

6. Deposit Shows You Want to Go vs. Dedication Shows You Want to Go. We usually request that youth make a commitment to a mission trip by a deposit or fee for a portion of the cost of the trip. Then, we require the rest of the fee long before the trip happens. Most youth groups I know have some sort of time in-between to do fundraising to help alleviate the cost of the trip. Paying a fee may show some signs that you want to go. However, I emphasize to my teens that dedication and commitment are actually the most important factors in showing your desire to go. Dedication or commitment to a mission trip means being faithful to attend mission meetings, do preparation (homework) between meetings as required by the leadership, and even participate in fundraising activities.

Colleagues in youth ministry who live in more affluent areas of the country often have parents of the teenagers willing to pay for the entire mission trip cost. However, as hinted at in the discussion of fundraising, this can come at the expense of teens (perhaps) being less dedicated to the trip.

In our youth group, we are clear about the expectations we have of our teens. We have a schedule of meetings. If teens and parents know they will miss more than two meetings, I tell them it is better not to sign up (and that maybe God has called them to something else that summer). Moreover, when they miss two meetings, we meet with the parents and teen to tell them that they will not be allowed to go on the STM if they miss another meeting. We also outline all fundraising team functions that are required as well as assignments that each teen will be given weekly. This can sound superficial compared to actually being dedicated in your *heart* to go on the trip. However, if teens are having difficulty doing these things, it is a good indicator of how lukewarm they are regarding an STM trip.

7. Deposit Reserves Your Spot vs. Dedication and Commitment Confirm Spot. Each and every teen and adult leader can make a deposit to go on an STM trip. We make sure to tell the parents it is a non-refundable deposit and, at the same time, it reserves the place for their child. While a family reserves a spot with a deposit, the dedication and commitment will be confirmed from the attitude of the participant in the STM trip. Some years ago, when we took our first trip to a difficult area in Africa, we interviewed teens to make sure their hearts were in the right place. However, we know it is difficult to assess teenagers. As resilient as teenagers are, some of them do step up when they are placed in the context of an STM team and some do not. Hence, I prefer to let teens apply and allow a few weeks for self-assessment. If the teen is not ready, I will talk to the parents and teenager very early in the process and return deposits as needed. What I try to emphasize to our youth and their parents is that we need to see continual efforts for the STM trip to confirm that the teen is willing to go. We want to nurture their commitment and dedication to their STM trip. It is the ultimate confirmation of how a teen values the mission.

8. Little or No Work vs. Hard Work, Homework, Heart Work.
When I go on a vacation, I do not expect to work. By definition, vacations should be no work or little work. The only work I want to do on a vacation is selecting what I am going to do that day or what I am going to eat. Contrast that with an STM trip. Teens need to be aware that they are going to be called to work.

In my years of attending many mission trips where other churches were involved, I can tell you that there is a difference between what I have seen in our teens versus others. I tell my teens that they need to have a "work hard, play hard" mentality. When it is time to work, it is time to *work*. There have been years where other church leaders have asked *our* youth to work with them. I value relationships and I am all for partnerships in ministry. However, I would appreciate it if other ministries instructed and taught their teens that an STM trip involves hard work. If I don't see a similar level of hard work in the teens, I talk to their leader first. I treat all teens in a respectable, loving, and relational way and would *never* rebuke a teen from another youth group. For my own youth, I have built a foundation on which to encourage and even rebuke them if they get lazy on an STM trip. But I don't have that relational capital with teens from other churches. Ultimately, my hope is that other church leaders would prepare their teens for hard work on STM trips as well. It is perhaps obvious, but something that can be neglected.

Hard work also involves STM team assignments. This means completing activities outside of the team meetings, which teens may call homework. This homework may involve simple Bible studies or journaling between team meetings. However, this is not just homework, but "heart work." One hope and goal of our STM trips is discipleship or more specifically, transformation in the lives of teens. That doesn't always happen before or during a trip. But at least we have a goal to plant seeds and promote a heart of service and discipleship in the lives of our youth. The STM trip is a great opportunity to cultivate a heart for Jesus and missions in the lives of the youth. Thus, "heart work" is important.

9. Fun for Me vs. Heart of Me. This is related to the last point. As a youth pastor, I have found that the STM trips are some of the most organic times of impromptu and hilarious fun, where memories are created for a lifetime and there is great joy. I think teens always look back upon a mission trip with some sort of positive memories, joy, and nostalgia. However, as I've said before, my ultimate goal is that the STM trip will be about the heart and spiritual life of each teen as well as impacting those they encounter. How God transforms each of our youth *and* others through this trip is the focus. I want teens to remember my hope for them.

10. Unity = Togetherness vs. Unity = United with/in Christ and His Purpose. I appreciate football, because I think it is the ultimate team sport. When I watched my son play varsity high school football, I could feel the team spirit. Often the team would rally around my son when he made a huge play. I saw in those moments that their unity was not just about the team being together or because of a uniform or team name. Rather, they were united for a purpose. I try to convey to our STM teams that we are united around a purpose. Due to the size of our youth group, we have mission trips to three or four different locations. I always say that we are "one team, different locations." This is partly because I do not want cliques to form in our youth group between the different teams.

However, this is also important because I want every youth group participant to know that what unites us is our purpose. And that purpose is to serve Christ and spread his gospel. I take the doctrine of Union with Christ seriously. I believe that every Christian is united to Christ, which subsequently means we are all united to each other through Christ, with Jesus Christ as our common and unifying bond. This doctrine helps us to also remember that every Christian we meet is part of the Body of Christ. Similarly then, teens can begin to see that the "church" is far bigger than their local church. I believe this helps them see a great picture of Christianity and their purpose for an STM trip. It is much greater than just one trip. And what unites all Christians together is Christ and his purpose for our lives.

It is worth mentioning here to be aware of cliques and dating issues that form on any STM team, which may hamper team unity. Christ does unite the team as one, but issues of cliques on any team can hinder the team. When teens are on the mission field, they can begin to resonate with certain teammates. Or, after living and breathing with each other for many days, some may get annoyed with others. Hence, cliques and tensions happen and can impact your team. Likewise, when romances form on teams, be aware of how it separates that couple away from others. There is an exclusivity that sometimes comes with dating, which affects the couple's ability to unite with the rest of the team. Just keep watch over these things and let teens know to be self-aware as you prepare them.

11. No Cares About Life vs. Cares About Life in Christ and Life of Others. People are allowed to be carefree and without worry on vacations. (This is probably near impossible for adults, especially in our world where we are so connected to the internet and our phones.) There are times when I enjoy not having a care about life or work. Again, like I noted, I take time for myself every day. However, when doing missions, we are being commissioned by Christ and called to serve others. So, our focus needs to be on Christ, our life in Christ, and the lives of others. We have a purpose for going on our STM trips and they are more than just social justice or humanitarian trips. We are going in the name and love of Christ, to love others.

12. No Cares About Our Actions vs. Action and Words Display Christ or the Opposite. Teenagers can be fun and live life to the fullest. It is important to let them display their individuality and personality. I value the uniqueness of each person and member of our youth group. However, when on an STM trip, our teens are not just there for themselves. I am amazed that often on domestic trips when we are in a certain location, the local television crews or newspapers will come out to take pictures and interview those of us who have come to serve. They are seeing the actions of these teenagers and the impact they are making. In addition, what is more amazing to the local television crews, it seems, is that teenagers are spending their summer break doing these things. Hence, it is evident that our actions (and words) display Christ.

Our dress, our actions, and our words can be an example for Christ or they can turn people away. In this way, for males and females, we emphasize modest dress. In more recent years, dress has been an issue of concern for many youth groups and churches I have encountered. Appropriate dress cannot be "suggestive" and must be culturally sensitive. Each church will need to make careful decisions in this regard for both genders. (See chapter eight for more.)

Our words also, especially swearing, must be considered with teens. I am not a legalistic and I have sworn a few times in anger. But teens swear sometimes just out of habit. I make them aware that in the mission field they are representing Christ and that their words must be guarded.

13. Once a Summer vs. Before and After the Summer. A vacation for many families may be once a summer or once a year. Some teenagers even get a vacation and then may get a few other weekend trips away with their parents. In this final point, I emphasize that the STM trip is not just a once-a-summer thing or an event. Missions are part of the youth group and church year round.

Missions simply must be part of a youth group's curriculum and year-round events. It should be taught about and occurring long before we go on a summer STM trip and continue to be a part of the ministry and the lives of teenagers long after.

SECTION III
BEING THERE: ON THE FIELD

CHAPTER 12 | AWARENESS WHILE ON THE TRIP

There are different things a group needs to be aware of while on the trip. Overall, short-term missionaries are representing Christ, and I believe that is the most important thing we need to be aware of. Even if you are bringing teens less mature in faith, part of the preparation before and what do you while you are on the STM trip will be representing Christ.

As I mentioned, for a few STM trips, either on our own or with a mission organization where we joined other churches, the local press has come to do a newspaper article or television news story about a group of teenagers coming to serve for a week. This is always encouraging and humbling to me, that the local media would make such a huge deal about our team. However, standing out and being an encouragement to a local community comes with responsibility. We are serving in the name of Jesus. Hence, awareness of our actions as an STM team is essential and needs to always be emphasized with our group.

As I noted in the second chapter, some of the sharpest critiques of STM trips are about the people/youth that go on them. Our group has these four mottos to help us remember why and what we are on the mission field for. These mottos are reminders and teachings for our youth as we prepare to interact with other people when on the mission trip. Moreover, these mottos keep teenagers grounded and focused on their purpose in being there, but also these mottos help prevent our teams from becoming insensitive, tourists, or "ugly

Americans" while on our STM trip. It is important to keep the youth aware of *what* they are doing and *how* they are acting on the STM trip, as ambassadors of Christ.

There is a reason why there are just four mottos. A few years ago, my youth ministry intern, Joshua Lee, succinctly packaged the four things we wanted our group to be aware of while on a mission trip. And it has made so much sense. They are easy to remember. Likewise, it is far easier to say "Motto One" to a teen (or out loud to our group), than repeat the whole motto while we are serving. Similarly, for the sake of those we are meeting on the mission field and ministering to, saying something like "Motto One" (or Two or Three, etc.) doesn't sound like I am chiding or rebuking our team. We just say "Motto One" and everyone hears it and can refocus.

THE MOTTOS

Below are the four mottos we use as we prepare for our STM trip and go over again during our mission trip, and after, and a little background on each. (Thank you, Joshua Lee.)

1. **Leave the place better than you found it.**
2. **Do not be near another youth group teen. Get involved with others.**
3. **If you find yourself idle, do something!**
4. **Love the Lord your God with all your heart, mind, soul, and strength.**

Motto 1: Leave the place better than you found it. This relates most to the "ugly American" idea but is a good rule for teenagers in general. Stereotypically, they are sloppy, messy, and do not clean up after themselves unless they learn it at home. Even then, when their parents are not around, anything can happen. When we do mission trips domestically, whether visiting a church to do VBS or some kind of construction, some of our teens make an area of work look like a war zone during the day. Whether it is a church, someone's home, or a public place, we want to be sensitive to the people who are welcoming and hosting us.

I noted earlier that we invite teenagers from our church to eat and have fellowship at our home often. It is always clearly evident which of them have learned how to clean up after themselves and which have not. I am not saying this to disrespect their parents or guardians. But some teenagers have not been taught this *effectively*.

A few years ago, while painting a kitchen for a family, the humidity was preventing paint from drying quickly. It caused quite a few drops of paint to drip. After we left the person's home for the night, I was called by the resident who complained of paint drops all over her floor. Fortunately, it was hardwood floors and we went back and did a good job removing any paint drops. However, the next day, I could see the loss of trust we had with the homeowner.

In working with host churches or missionaries overseas, I have heard first-hand about teams coming and not cleaning up after themselves. It then became the job of the host churches or missionaries to be butlers and cleaning ladies. Instead of supporting their work, more work was created and time was taken away from their missionary efforts.

Throughout the day of serving, we continue to say to the group and each other "Motto One." It reminds us that in serving others, leaving the place better than we found it is a great testimony to the love and care of Christ.

Motto 2: Do not be near another youth group teen. Get involved with others. I hope these mottos do not sound tyrannical. However, in regard to "Motto Two," I have found that even the most outgoing teenagers, when tossed into new situations, can easily resort to their comfort zones. This means talking and socializing with each *other* instead of those we came to serve.

Over the years, our youth group has done youth camps on mission trips—for the sake of evangelizing as well as encouraging the churches we have been sent to. It is basically like doing a youth retreat. And most of the international youth groups and youth pastors we have encountered have very little experience in the "fun" aspect of retreats. They are accustomed to just gathering and teaching their group.

This ministry has enabled our youth group teenagers to go overseas, to meet teenagers/peers, and to share the gospel with non-believers or encourage other Christians with wild and fun games. One might blame a language barrier for this, but overall, when meeting new people, some of our teenagers have simply gotten shy or tentative. We use "Motto Two" to encourage our team to move *outward* and away from their own mission team members.

Even on domestic trips doing VBS or construction on a person's home, we are also there to share our lives. I tend to see teens, especially in the early days of arriving at a new place, congregate towards each other or just be shy and not engage with those we are meeting. Just saying "Motto Two" out loud reminds them when they are too close to each other and not getting involved enough with others.

Motto 3: If you find yourself idle, do something! I love my youth. I have been a youth pastor for over 26 years—22 at my present church. So, I say this with love. On any STM trip, especially in the summer, it can get hot. Towards the end of an STM trip, our teens get tired. Even if you have been good about rest and sleep, the team gets tired. When they get physically hot or when they get tired, their tendency is to become idle (i.e., *lazier*). This is just my experience. Other times, they are just sitting around talking to each other (reinforce Motto Two) or lounging.

I always feel terrible about this when we are overseas with missionaries, who are often so humble in their care for us. And sometimes missionaries who our church supports have expressed the desire to treat our STM teams well so our church would continue to support them. I feel uneasy when they have those fears. I see them doing things for our team to make *us* comfortable. When I see the missionary's efforts to love our team, I get upset if I see our team lounging around or being lazy. Of course, I don't want to show my irritation, so saying "Motto Three" is a great way to tell the group to "get off their butts!" right now.

Motto 4: Love the Lord your God with all your heart, mind, soul, and strength. This is more of a general thing that we remind the group of all the time during our trip. We want these teens, even the less mature or unchurched teens in our group, to always know why we are on the STM trip. Likewise, we want our team to remember that God is the center and impetus for the STM trip. It's part theological, part pedagogical, but after all is said and done, we are on a Christian-/church-based mission trip. We are not going just to feel good about ourselves, for community service hours, or because social justice is the new rage. We are serving because God loves us and we are called to love him and others with all our hearts, minds, souls, and strength.

Likewise, in chapter 10, when I discussed preparing teens for difficult food situations, or teaching them about being culturally sensitive through humility, openness, and having a learner's heart—these all fall under "Motto Four." It is meant to be general, to encompass the heart posture of each team member, as we have prepared them for the STM trip and as they participate in the trip itself.

In the end, in considering our mottos, your group could add more or have more profound ones. There are many things I want my teens to be aware of, and I've discussed how I prepare our youth in chapters 10 and 11. Likewise, we are continuing to remind them of the mottos and things like reactions to new foods, for example, *throughout* the trip.

Having these four core concepts, however, so succinctly packaged into mottos, does summarize for me the most important things I want our teens to be aware of on the trip. (Likewise, as I noted before, it sounds better to say "Motto Three" than "Stop being a lazy jerk.") Finally, our awareness while we are on the trip is for a greater purpose. It is to model and exhibit God's love for others.

CHAPTER 13 | CONTINGENCIES AND THE UNEXPECTED

There are times when the unexpected happens on an STM trip. I had shared in the introduction that one of our STM team teenagers, sadly, drowned and died in 1995, although I was not on that mission trip. I don't think there is any way to prepare for that tragic contingency. My close friend David Larry (yes, that is his name) who is a youth worker in Florida, also lost a youth group member in a drowning accident just a few years ago. After he came back, I was one of the few people who could relate to him, comfort him, and give him some advice on how to handle the situation at church and with parents. However, we never talked about such a scenario before he went on his STM trip. In fact, why would we talk about such a sad topic? Though he's now in heaven, today I am encouraged that the testimony of his student Joshua's life has become a hope for many. There has been a foundation started in his name, to help the same people he served in South America. However, this particular situation is something I believe no youth worker normally could or would want to talk about before an STM trip.

There are some contingencies and unexpected scenarios that do happen on an STM trip, though, that are a little more common. This chapter will outline some examples and suggest what to do when/ if they occur. Still, there are so many hypotheticals that it is hard to discuss every one. All the same, I will highlight a few in this chapter that have actually occurred a few times in my years of STM trips.

"THIS IS MISSIONS"

I say this on every mission trip: "It's not a mission trip unless something bad happens." This reminds me of my first year in Haiti and meeting the missionaries on the ground who hosted many different teams from the US during those first months after the earthquake. They would say "T.I.M."—which stood for "This Is Missions"—whenever something went wrong. This sentiment has been around in various forms for decades, usually used by British and American ex-patriots living abroad in cultures that are constantly shaking up their western view of "normal." A common variation of the phrase was referenced in the movie *Blood Diamond,* when one character says, "T.I.A" or "This Is Africa." It's a saying that marks adjusted expectations—things often don't go as planned when we are in an unfamiliar culture.

I like what the phrase communicates because, on the mission field, things *don't* always go as planned and there *will* be contingencies and unexpected turns. Hence, whether traveling overseas or domestically, preparing for the unexpected has always been important for my STM trips. Now, I know we can't plan for every emergency, contingency, or unexpected happening on the mission field. However, having some well-thought-out plans for various scenarios can be helpful.

With that in mind, here is list of suggestions:

Have emergency contacts ready back home. There need to be people identified back home who are ready to receive your call if you have any emergencies, and you need to have their information on you— and on other adult leaders—during the trip. A few summers back, one of our vehicles was broken down during a trip. It was nice to have someone at home to contact about the situation who could be proactive in communicating with church leaders and help us search for places where we could fix the problem. I could have searched the internet myself, but when you are at the mission site, "the show must go on." Despite there being other leaders, it was helpful for me to be able to focus on what needed to be done for the mission and have someone at home help arrange the things needed to fix our vehicle.

Emergency contacts should also have copies of all passports, your travel information, and at least one should serve as a point person for parents curious about the happenings of the trip. I always have one person who can serve in this role and, conversely, can contact me if there are any emergencies back at home that someone on our team needs to know about.

Have emergency contacts ready in your locale. On domestic trips, knowing the location of the ER or even the local Walmart is very important. These are the two most vital things I can think of. In case small emergencies or needs arise, you can find a lot of things at Walmart or a similar type store.

If you are overseas where a local missionary lives year round, they will probably have any very basic emergency information you might want to leave with your stateside emergency contact person and also have with you on the trip—information like the local hospital and American embassy phone numbers. A professional mission organization (domestic or overseas) has already been on the ground and knows the area. If an emergency happens, they will know what to do, and you can ask them in advance if you want the information with you. Their ability to readily solve problems in emergency situations is probably one of the best reasons to partner with them.

Know what to do about lost luggage. If you are flying domestically or overseas, luggage will get lost once in a while. When luggage is lost, you and your team will be the last ones left around the conveyor belt. Just think about how you are going to handle a group of teenagers in this scenario. Likewise, you and the teen who lost his or her luggage will have to report the missing luggage, hand over your baggage claim ticket/number, file a report, and give an address where the luggage can be sent. (This is where those pre-made labels for the airline luggage tags come in handy again. You can quickly give the destination address where you will be staying.)

One more thing about luggage being lost, it means the T.I.M. principle goes into effect. Moreover, it will mean that someone in your team may be without clothes for a few days and perhaps even the whole trip. In overseas locations, the luggage may arrive a few days later but going back to the airport or getting it delivered to the place you are staying may be difficult. If we assess that a team member will probably not be able to get back their luggage or we know they won't for the duration of the trip, I call into action our team unity in Christ. I ask team members of the same gender to each donate one shirt, one pair of pants, and one clean under garment. It doesn't sound appealing, but it is a good way for everyone to help. Moreover, it's very helpful to the person who lost their luggage, as they don't have to scrounge each day to find clothes. Of course, the person who borrows all the clothes is charged with washing and returning the clothes as well. I want to emphasize again that losing your luggage is stressful for anyone. Yet, if others can work together to help, it relieves a long-term issue for the trip and for the person whose luggage has been lost.

Have a plan in case a van/car breaks down. When one of your vehicles breaks down, especially if your youth group is caravanning to a location, you have to think about what to do. One year, after driving eight hours home, our van broke down two hours from church at a rest stop. It was getting late, and I was worried we would not make it back home. This may sound crazy, but I had the team march around the van seven times (like before the fall of Jericho) and pray. And you know what, I would not be telling you this story if the van hadn't actually started!

But when a vehicle does break down, you really do have to think about what to do. You can't just march around it and hope for the best. And in my story from many years ago, I had no idea what to do besides pray (desperately). Do you leave the team members behind in the broken-down vehicle? Do you just leave the driver, try to fit everyone into the other vehicles, and travel ahead? Do you all just wait to get the vehicle repaired? There are many factors that will go into this decision. For example: the time of day, how close you are to your destination, and how long it may take to repair the vehicle. These are all things to be aware of. Of particular note, when caravanning home, it is always nice for all the vehicles to show up back at your church together, if possible. I believe it gives parents and those at church a sense that your team was unified and organized.

Be flexible when there are missed connections. When flying, be aware that there is always a chance for missed connections, especially weather related in the summer. Be aware that rebooking tickets for an entire group—as previously discussed—is tricky, as airlines have less availability on flights now. I like to discuss some of these scenarios beforehand—especially if you are traveling with teenagers and your group cannot be rebooked on another flight together. In this case, you probably do not want to send a group of teenagers by themselves. Mention this scenario in your preparation with your adult leaders. Equip your adults to be ready in this situation. For our group, I make sure our adults know who may stay behind and who would go ahead, depending on how/if our group splits up.

Be prepared to handle inappropriate behavior. Before you go on your trip, I believe it is crucial to consider how you are going to deal with inappropriate behavior of teens. Minor incidents such as teenagers not respecting curfew or having bad attitudes is not what I have in mind here. These can be dealt with on the trip. While we have prepared our youth spiritually, mentally, and physically, there is always a risk of inappropriate behavior. This reminds me of what I noted earlier in the book, about how sometimes for youth groups, STM trips have become about an outreach to unchurched teens versus an experience for spiritually mature teens. Hence, sometimes, less spiritually mature youth may be attending your STM trip. Thus, thinking through how you may deal with inappropriate behavior is important.

As I noted earlier, you should have an emergency contact person back at home, so you can discuss any major incidents where you may have to send a teen home. Moreover, you will need to keep your church leadership abreast of any of these situations. I have never had to send a teenager home from a mission trip. The closest I have gotten is when two youth became attracted to each other on a trip. They were spending a lot of time with each other. One night, one of them decided to try to sneak out and meet the other person. Fortunately, I am the lightest sleeper ever. This however, happened again a few days later and the teen was getting extremely indignant, and it was not edifying for the team. I was spending so much time talking and ministering to this young person and taking time away from the rest of the team.

In extreme cases like this, I do think it would sometimes be best for the parents to come and get their children. I wound up not doing that in this particular situation, but it is always good to think about how you will deal with inappropriate behavior. In addition, so that parents are not caught off guard, it is our practice to tell parents during the initial meetings that, if needed, we *will* send teens home and it will be at their cost.

Be prepared for homesickness. Believe it or not, some teenagers may become homesick, even on a short STM trip. I think it is often because they are not used to being without the comforts and amenities of home. I know some teenagers are used to sleeping with their iPods and then go on an STM trip and cannot sleep. Just be aware that for those traveling away from home for the first time, there may be some homesickness for the comforts of home—or even simply their parents.

CHAPTER 14 | DAILY SPIRITUAL LIFE, DEBRIEFS, AND DIFFICULTIES

While on the mission trip, the day-by-day existence of your team is an important factor that needs to be intentionally thought about. I believe it's extremely important to have daily meetings with your team, preferably each morning and evening. STM trips away from home can be a tremendous opportunity for the spiritual growth and nurture of your team. The teens are away from family, away from distractions, and are focused for the most part on the STM trip and hopefully their faith. Likewise, there may be times of difficulty and hardship for some teens who are away from home. Again, I suggest holding meetings each morning and each evening to help them grow through the ups and downs of the experience.

MORNING MEETINGS

Whether on a domestic or overseas trip, in the morning meetings, we begin with some sort of team devotional or sharing from God's Word and sing a song or two of worship. What we have found extremely beneficial is rotating this responsibility among our team members (including our teenagers). This has really encouraged our entire team as each teen (rather than just the adults) shares his or her thoughts and reflections from the Word of God.

At the end of each sharing time, we do find it helpful for one of the adult leaders to summarize and put it into the context of the mission. Similarly, if the teen is capable of doing so, we do promote discussion time and allow them to facilitate it. If the person is not equipped for that, the adult can do it.

At the conclusion of this time, we usually spend some time in prayer. Afterward, we do lay out an agenda for the day, so our group is clear on what we are doing and what we are trying to accomplish. Of course, in many years of working with teenagers, I know that there will still be many in my group who ask during that day: "What are we doing next?" However, I do see the important value in laying out a clear vision for each day with the team.

EVENING MEETINGS AND REFLECTION

Each evening, we have a time of sharing again from the Word (again, from one of the teens if possible), as well as a time to debrief, pray, share group reflections and any additional teaching from Scripture, and have teens share from their journals or share what they thought of during the guided time of reflection. If your team is big, you may want to consider small groups for this.

Please understand, especially for our evening meetings, it is an art and not a science. In other words, while I have some structure and agenda in mind for our evening meeting, I say from experience that it's important to be more "flexible" during this meeting. Your group may be extremely tired from a long day of work. You may not want to let it drag on and on into a long meeting. I would trust that each youth worker would know their group and how much they can digest or take. Or, on the other hand, something could happen, and you may need to change the direction of your evening meeting. For example, someone may share something deep, and it could trigger an important discussion or great emotion.

I think my ultimate goal for the evening meetings is to process the day through the Word and a time of sharing from the group. I want to encourage and guide them as they consider how the day was or, more generally, have a purposeful time of reflection and, as time or context permits, to give a glimpse near the end of our meeting of what is going on the next day.

I know there have been days when the local community children we did VBS with came back to play with our teens. It distracted our group in a positive way, and I wasn't going to hold even a 45-minute meeting that night after our group spent so much energy playing with these children—I also knew I could do the next morning what I planned to discuss that evening. At other times, after experiencing a powerful moment that day, teens want to process and talk about it no matter how tired they are. I remember vividly our second day in Haiti on our second trip there. Seeing the rampant devastation of a remote village, our teenagers started reflecting on brokenness and despair. Moreover, suddenly we broke out in a chorus of "How He Loves Us" by David Crowder in that moment of vulnerability and fatigue. We must have sang that song for almost an hour with times of passionate prayer mixed in-between. It was really quite powerful and transformative. I wasn't going to just end that meeting because they had to go to sleep or stick with a prepared Bible study just because I'd prepared one. I think, ultimately, it is important to prepare and have a general plan of what each morning and evening may look like, but it is far more important to be flexible and discern what your teens need.

Still, I have found that at the end of the day, having a regular time for reflection is a great time of spiritual growth for the team. It will be up to you to think about how you want to structure this each night, depending on your team. Yet, as I noted, be flexible. In Section V, I offer some suggestions. However, in considering the pedagogies of learning that STM trips can provide for our youth, as noted in chapter three, the value of doing this is really important. Yet, all the time—I will say it again—be flexible, be sensitive to the Holy Spirit. In other words, pay attention to your team and how God may be leading you.

BEYOND MEETINGS

During each day of the mission trip, there may be moments of down time and even boredom. It's important to guide your group just enough so that they have free time but aren't spending it in ways that aren't edifying.

This boredom can be especially felt because on our mission trips, we ask them not to bring media devices and phones, as I mentioned previously. Most are used to taking pictures on their phones a lot, and some will welcome the chance to help document the trip, if asked. If, as suggested earlier, you assign a few teens the chore of taking photos or shooting videos for the team, those missing their phones for pictures will know they can request a few specific pictures each day if needed, alleviating some of that no-phone anxiety/boredom.

Another side note to this, if you chose to allow your photographers or any of your youth to bring their own cameras, which may be high tech, those cameras can become just as much of a distraction as the phones would have been. Especially if they feel tech-deprived without their phones, some teens will use the camera to satisfy their need to have electronics. They will huddle around their camera to look at the pictures taken of the day or the trip, hunkering down with the tech instead of participating. It becomes their "phone" and a distraction in and of itself. Hence, I just try to have one or two photographers for the team.

To help alleviate general boredom, bring along some games like Uno, Monopoly Deal, and even playing cards—or whatever easy-to-transport games your group enjoys. In addition, these games are a great way for your teens to interact with each other in ways that otherwise may never happen outside a mission trip. With these games, you do have to make sure that people are participating in them or it could become an exclusive activity as well.

I've mentioned the need for journals, in part, because journaling is another way to help your teens pass time on a mission trip, but it's also a great and productive exercise for them. As a leader, you can give them some guidelines or let them write about what they want. However, it can be powerful simply as a more personal reflection for each of them. We also ask our teens to share from their journals at our group meetings, so many of our girls and guys are more inclined to write in them. We also promote opportunities to journal each evening about the past day and each morning after a night of sleep. Our groups in the past have purchased small, inexpensive notebooks for the teens or you can utilize something like the Interactive Journal.

On the latter part of the trip, we also ask the youth to write encouragement notes to other team members and anybody they wish to write to that they have served with during the trip. This includes people at the mission trip location, such as local leaders or people who have hosted our team. This has been a great activity, writing these encouragement notes to each other, and the notes are something they each take home and cherish. They also serve as great reminders and remembrances of the trip. (As discussed earlier, one consideration about writing notes to local people is telling your team whether or not to give out personal information such as home addresses and phone numbers.)

WATCHING OVER TEENS

Difficulties for teens can arise on an STM trip, and it's something to be aware of and sensitive to as an adult leader. Even on a short mission trip, for some adolescents, being away from home can be a time of difficulty and stress. For example, waking up in a sleeping bag or air mattress for days can be uncomfortable. Not having the comforts of foods you are accustomed to or mom or dad around you can be hard. In this way, I look for signs of when a teen might be homesick and other signs of sadness. This may sound ridiculous, but don't forget that you are on an STM mission trip and doing God's work. In other words, while I don't expect to wake up seeing Satan next to me, I am constantly reminded of 1 Peter 5:8 when doing STM work. It says, "Be alert and of sober mind. Your enemy the devil prowls around like a roaring lion looking for someone to devour." Nowhere does this seem truer than on an STM trip. In addition, we must be aware of this as we consider our teens and their emotional/spiritual well-being.

Food and drink is another consideration as far as difficulties for adolescents. While I believe that teenagers are resilient, especially physically, we need to look out for their well-being in new environments and encourage or advise them accordingly. As discussed in chapter 10, whether you are in the US or abroad, the physical exertion and the foods you encounter (or lack thereof) can be a challenge, even if the teens have been mentally prepared ahead of time. While some teens may just eat well without prompting, others may not. Along these lines of eating and digestion, when teenagers are in a new environment, their bathroom habits may get affected too, especially bowel movements. For example, for some, just seeing a different type of bathroom may cause them to not go to the bathroom as regularly. Believe me, this is something that you need to be aware of and look out for. See how they are eating on the trip. Consider how they are feeling physically. Moreover, if they are not going to the bathroom as regularly as they do at home, this can pose a problem.

These words may seem unnecessary now, if you've never travelled with your students. But, unlike summer camp, where many churches have access to a camp nurse or medic, you and your leaders will likely be the frontline of care for the physical needs of your kids on a mission trip. You and your adult leaders simply need to be sensitive in watching over the teens and discerning and wise in helping them function the best they can in new and unusual circumstances.

SECTION IV
BACK AGAIN: HOME LIFE

CHAPTER 15 | COMING HOME

Whether a domestic trip or international trip, whether flying home or taking a long drive, I can remember going on mission trips as a teenager and coming home. My youth pastor would always say to be careful, as Satan is ready to devour us like roaring lion. (There's 1 Peter 5:8 again.) I did not heed these words as much as I should have. But I do remember what it was like to come home from various trips—and one trip, in particular. We were so excited to be going home, our team was all crazy and hyped. We were screaming and shouting in the van. The hype and celebration was real. But in fact, one of our team members nearly got hit by another van passing by because they were so hyped to be going home, they were not paying attention to their surroundings in the rest-stop parking lot.

The last few days of the trip, it is important to prepare your group for the journey home. Traveling home from the mission trip poses many interesting scenarios. Teenagers are usually excited, but some of course are not. In addition, unpacking your team's experiences coming home from spiritually and mentally invigorating or difficult trips is also important. In these last two chapters, we are going to be talking about coming home from a mission trip and some important factors to consider for your teenagers.

Coming home from Costa Rica two decades ago, we arrived in Miami for our connecting flight home to Philadelphia. I sent the team ahead to the gate where our connection flight was leaving from. I needed to make a call (it was 1996, before the age of the modern cell phone) to make sure our ride was coming to the airport to pick us up. Of course, a few adults led them to the gate. As I was walking to the gate, I heard a gate change and went to the new gate, assuming the team would be there or at least on their way there. When I got to the new gate, I didn't see anyone. I walked back to the original gate and didn't see them there either. As time was approaching to board our flight, I was getting scared. About five minutes before the plane doors closed, I saw a pack of teenagers and adults running down the terminal, which was of course our team. When I asked one of the adults what happened, they said the teens were getting pizza and ice cream and somehow no one noticed the gate for the flight was moved.

I assume that this was just a problem of that era and would never happen in our age of instant communication via cell phones. However, I think there is a phenomenon, whether driving or flying back home, that you are "coming home!" There is some kind of extreme joy and excitement that both teenagers and adults experience, and it can become a distraction or blind spot that leads to miscommunication and mishaps.

PREPARE YOUR YOUTH TO GO HOME

Hence, as an experienced youth pastor and veteran of many STM trips, I believe some preparation in this area is worth noting. There is nothing wrong with your team being hyped and excited to come home. But I do warn teens of a few things before the trip *and* as we are traveling home.

Remind your team it's not over yet. I half-jokingly tell our team, "The mission trip doesn't end until you get into your parents car." It is, again, a half-joke, but I'm also making sure the group knows the *trip* part of the mission does not end until they are back in their parents' cars safe and sound. They need to be alert and aware all the way until they get there.

Remind your team of what *God* has done. I like to remind them of all the great work they did on the trip as we prepare to go home and as we are traveling, and how God "used" them for his purposes.

I emphasize the word *used* to express that God's great work was done by God, through them, for his purposes. This is my subtle but important reminder that God has done all the work. I do not want to take away from the great work these teens have done. I want to encourage them, that they are God's workmanship created in Christ to do the work of God, as Ephesians 2:10 says. But it is a subtle reminder and my way of keeping them humble and focused. They need to be subdued in their (perhaps) unconscious celebrations that "I am all that" and "I did such great work." When we think "I" did something, we forget the Author and Perfector of the mission trip. We can easily go from being humble and grateful to thinking "I did great and now I can just go crazy and enjoy myself."

Overall, I think it is effective to just spiritually and mentally prepare the team for the journey home. It grounds them and gives them some sense that they are still on the mission trip as they go home and also long after. You can probably come up with your own thoughts, theology, and practices to accomplish this. However, my purpose is to harness and balance the great joy and excitement of teenagers as they go home.

Remind your team how to travel well. A quick run-through of your travel plan, your airport (or road trip) dos and don'ts, and your expectations of the group will be key for a good trip home. Everyone will be tired, but putting as much care and consideration into the trip home as you put into the trip there is important.

PREPARE YOURSELF AND YOUR LEADERS TOO
The reality is that while you and your volunteer leaders have maturity on your side, you might actually be more tired than the teenagers and even more excited to get home, so it's important for you and your leadership team to finish strong.

Here are some things I've learned that might help:

Remember to leave the mission field well. As you prepare to come home, do not forget to consider how you will keep nurturing your ongoing relationship with the people you have served with on the mission field. This can be relationships with organizations and churches you have served with on a domestic trip. Or it can be the missionaries you served with overseas. Whoever you partnered with, before you say goodbye, begin to talk through and investigate with them how you may support them in the future or what you can do better in future STM trips with them or in general.

Finally, establish clear ways you will communicate and continue your relationships with them. On a side note, it is always nice to give them a call or email when you arrive back home. They will probably be praying for you and will miss you after you and your team leave. Of course, if they don't, it is probably a sign you are not invited back. (Kidding. Sort of.)

Remember you are responsible for precious lives. I always remind myself and other adult leaders that we are taking care of other people's children. And as we prepare to go home, our job isn't done yet either. I believe that this care is a huge responsibility. Frankly, for some younger youth workers, the weight of this—though important—may not be as heavy. I will admit that as a younger youth pastor, I really despised when parents pulled the "you just don't understand, you don't have children/teenagers" card on me. I do believe youth workers care and in many ways love and understand our teenagers, regardless of whether or not we have children or teenagers of our own. However, I embrace the important reality that these parents or guardians have permitted me to take their children, their teenagers on a trip for a week or two, have invested a lot of time into it, and in many cases these parents have high hopes for the spiritual growth and change in their teenagers' lives.

I guess what I am ultimately saying is, I want to make sure these teenagers get back to their homes safely. As a leader then, it is up to me and our other adults to prepare ourselves and our teenagers to make it back home. Perhaps because—as I discussed in the introduction of this book—my colleague once had the terrible experience of having to face a parent whose son had drowned while on the mission trip he led. It is almost a traumatic aftershock for me still to this day. Soberly speaking, I believe it is crucially important and want to stress that the journey home is not a time to get sloppy or careless, no matter how tired we are.

Remember to think through details of your travel home. If you are flying or driving within the US, go back over all the details that got you to your location safely—or consider mistakes that were made and how to fix them—then be sure you are prepared to get your group home.

When heading back home to America from an overseas location, there will be certain travel-related issues you need to remember. Many of these overlap with the same points I made in chapter six regarding flying as a team. But I think it is noteworthy to highlight these one last time, because you are traveling with a group of teenagers.

> **Passports.** If you travelled internationally, these are crucial. Sometimes they are checked both at security and the gate. Always have them ready.

> **Customs.** Again, for international flights, make sure you and your group know what to expect and how to behave during this portion of travel.

> **Pick-Up Times.** Delayed flights (international *or* domestic, by the way), picking up checked bags, going through customs, or simply a busy runway can all interfere with the time your team is ready to be picked up. Be sure you have communicated the need for flexibility and have a way to communicate delays.

ONCE YOU'RE BACK

Eventually the issues of the trip home will be dealt with, the last teen will be picked up, and you will be back to the comforts of home and the familiar. But there are two things you'll want to be prepared for:

1. Set aside time to rest and recuperate once the team is safe at

home. I would like to state that when you do get home, as the adult leader, you need some rest. I know that if you're a volunteer or bi-vocational youth worker, you may not have this luxury. You may have to go back to work. But if you are on staff at a church, you should have the option of time off—or you may need to lobby for it.

I would say that on an STM mission trip of one week, for example, you are basically spending all 168 hours living, breathing, and tending to the teenagers on your team. There are not too many breaks. Hence, after returning from an STM trip and embracing my huge responsibility to get them home, I usually take a few days to do *nothing*. I mean, an STM trip with teens is basically like doing approximately three weeks of full time ministry in just seven days. Hence, once you are back, advise your church that you have really not had any Sabbath rest from ministry for 168 hours (or whatever number applies) and help them understand you need some sort of break after the trip. It's important. Plan for this before you go and protect the time when you return.

2. Be prepared to report on your mission. Back in the early 1990s, I can still remember the painstaking effort that one of my youth ministry mentors went through to do a mission report to the church after the youth group returned from an STM trip. He would take all the mission trip pictures, develop them, then choose the ones he thought would best express and show what the STM team had done on the mission trip. Then he would have to take those pictures and make them into slides (if you don't know what actual slides or a slide projector are, don't worry about it). Not only that, but he would painstakingly put them in order to create a nice slide show, while coordinating with a tape cassette or CD player to play some background music. Then he would have to turn on the music, while holding a microphone to it to amplify the sound, and click the slides in coordination with the music. All the while he would be narrating into another microphone. Today, we have iMovie to take care of all that.

Thank God.

Still, with all that work, my mentor Steve was great at presenting and reporting about the mission trip in an A/V format for our church. He would choose one of those great musical themes from a movie like *The Mission* to play alongside that slide presentation and the presentation became even more grand. His voice was also so majestic and powerful. His presentations made me want to cry and go on mission trips the next year. And I was just one of many feeling this. Even if people could not go the following year, if parents and church leaders saw his mission reports, these presentations ensured that the mission committee would give financial support for future teams and missionaries they supported around the world. (My mentor Steve was awesome!)

Of all things I learned from Steve, I learned the great importance and power of mission reports. Paul in the book of Acts always did mission reports to the church in Antioch when he returned, to further his mission work in the future. For your STM team, the mission report to your church congregation, leadership, parents, mission board, etc., is what will fuel and sustain your short-term mission efforts and vision for the future. Without them, you are going to fight uphill battles within your church as years go by. However, with them, the road can be easier. They can effectively "sell" the future of STMs for your youth group. Ultimately, as you are coming home and are home, mission reports are some of the most effective ways to show your church not only what the youth group experienced but also to endorse future efforts for STM trips.

Here are some things we do:

We find a day and time when we can make a congregational report to our church with the widest audience—and make sure any person related to our mission trip can be present. I want to make sure we can share with as many people as possible.

We create an effective A/V mission presentation. In our age of media and technology, it is easy and helpful to create a "highlight" video of your STM trip for church and youth group. Just one warning, since it is so easy to create videos these days, and I know some churches and youth ministries use video all the time. I really think about how to be strategic and effective with our A/V presentations. Since our church sends out multiple STM teams each year, we have to be wise about how and when we use media. Church members can get fatigued after watching what can—at our church anyway—turn out to be as many as eight mission trip videos a year. So, sometimes I like to mix it up when it comes to our presentation format. Verbal and written STM trip testimonies can be just as effective as a video, which brings me to the next step we take…

We have at least one teen per mission team share a brief but profound testimony live during the mission report. These testimonies are always powerful, as the Holy Spirit leads. They are effective in communicating to the entire congregation how God is using the teens and the youth group. They also help to endorse future STM trips for our youth.

We find forums in which to write up the testimonies and share pictures after the mission report as well. For you, these might be church newsletters, the youth website, church bulletin in future weeks, etc. We also make sure to send them to the parents and supporters of our STM trip.

CHAPTER 16 | LIVING AT HOME

One year, as we began registration for our upcoming summer mission trips, my wife had what is still a vivid conversation with a teen. This girl was repeatedly saying that she could not wait to go on the STM trip that year. When my wife probed more deeply, the girl kept saying it was because she missed the feeling of being on the mission trip. *She missed the feeling.* These words continue to stick with me today (as well as the lyrics to the song "You Lost That Loving Feeling") and it is why what happens after the mission trip (and before, as a matter of fact) is just as important as what we do during it.

The book of James says faith without works is dead. For me, one particular application of this passage is that I believe, for Christians, if we are not practicing our faith in action and deed, our faith will seem like it is dying. An illustration of "faith and good works" is often given in terms of taking steps walking forward. You take one step with your left foot (faith), then right foot (good works) to keep moving forward. However, if you don't do both, if you only take steps with one foot, you become stuck in one place.

This teen I mentioned had had such a great experience on the mission trip the previous summer. She did amazing work and was a great part of our team. But after the trip, her Christian experience was never quite as powerful as what she experienced on the STM trip. Consequently, she was struggling in her faith.

These kinds of stories scare me. They *really* scare me. Not only was she letting her faith journey be defined by an experience and feeling, but she had functioned for many months after our trip not being able to experience that "high" from the mission trip. Frankly speaking, the STM trip had become like a drug for her, and it seemed she had used it to get a high she couldn't get in her daily Christian life.

PERSPECTIVE AT HOME

There is another term for what the girl was going through, which I have heard and borrowed from various colleagues over the years. It is PMS or Post-Mission Syndrome. It may not be the most politically correct term and may be insensitive to females, so I apologize for the name. What this terminology connotes, however, is important regardless of the uncomfortable initials. It is the idea of a time period after mission trips when adolescents—and sometimes adults too—get spiritually fatigued and more (or less) emotional about their mission trip, but also (more devastatingly) about their spiritual life and the vibrancy of it.

Much of what is written about STMs highlights the importance of incorporating STM trips and a theology of mission into the whole life and practice of the youth group. It must move away from just being an event or program in the summer. In this way, STM trips become most effective. Hence, the "living at home" aspect of the mission trip must be incorporated into your overall STM trip plans, including after the trip and as part of the whole youth group ministry. For our group, during STM preparation and while on the STM trip itself, we are constantly talking about how our youth group can and will do "missions" long after the trip, as part of the entire youth ministry philosophy.

In addition, to help combat any STM-related post-mission syndrome, we promote *two* key ideas with our youth during the last few days of the mission trip as well as once all our mission teams return back home. We are also constantly making these ideas part of our preparation before we go our mission trip. Moreover, we hammer these ideas in on the final days and after we return home (and I probably say these things year round at youth group too). In fact, it is important that your mission trip preparation and meetings *include* post-mission-trip meetings that are accounted for and scheduled as thoroughly as possible at the onset of your STM trip preparation. (You'll see in Section V, Act III on page 303 what types of meetings can be productive and effective after you return from your STM trip.)

Anyway, these two ideas/teachings are as follows:

1. "The mission starts at home, when we return." The final days of the mission trip, as well as post-mission-trip follow-up meetings are littered with this statement and teaching on it. We want to promote the idea that missions is not just the few days you spend going somewhere but is a lifelong calling for every believer. Moreover, while STMs can be for the glory of God, 1 Corinthians 10:31 clearly states that *all* things can be for the glory of God. Hence whether on an STM trip or after an STM trip, *all* is for the glory of God. This means daily school work, life at home, relationships, youth group meetings… you name it.

We also emphasize throughout that both local and overseas missions are important and one should not be neglected over the other. Hence, home, your neighborhood, and your local school are all mission fields. Years ago, I heard a Chuck Swindoll sermon where he talked about missions. I can't recall his exact words, but he said something along the lines of this: "Before you go across the sea, go across the street."[1] I love that. But I made my own extension of that quote. I have said in many messages and sermons: "Before you go across the sea, go across the street. And before you go across the street, go across the seats." The seats! What I am talking about is that even within our church "seats" there is a lot of mission work we can do on a daily basis. Of course, that includes our teenagers being involved and serving within the youth ministry also.

In this way, a theology and practice of missions must be fully incorporated into your mission trip and your youth group ministry. The STM trip must be just *one* way to do "missions" in the youth group. Similarly, year-round effort to do missions must be developed and implemented in your youth group. As I stated at the beginning of the book, in our youth group, we try to make sure that we are on board with this each season. There is not a season (or three months) that goes by that our youth group is not doing some sort of mission work. Moreover, throughout the year, I have brought in speakers to talk about their lives and faith in their workplaces. Again, these have included doctors, lawyers, teachers, business people, orchestra conductors, chefs, etc. It is vital for our youth to see that an effective STM trip is just one part of a church. But a church must always be seeking to "gather," as I noted in chapter one.

One great resource for this that you can use in your final days as you prepare to come back home and when you return is a blog post called "Six Ways to Reach God's World" from OMF (Overseas Missionary Fellowship).[2] It gives an overview of ways people can reach God's world, including the "going" aspect, which your STM trip has done. However, this resource frames "reaching God's world" as not only the "going" part, but also the learning, praying, sending, welcoming, and mobilizing parts too. These are all aspects of missions that our youth can continue in long after their "short-term" experiences.

2. "Our final home is in heaven." Revelation 21:1-4 talks about the new heaven and new earth. These verses have deep meaning to me, especially since losing my dad who had a difficult struggle with cancer many years ago. In fact, any believer who has lost a loved one can embrace these verses. They are verses for all believers and should be a hopeful message of our final and ultimate home. Similarly, the passage should give us an eternal perspective of this life, our purpose on earth, and the fact that we will be secure with Jesus in our final home someday. Moreover, it gives Christians full assurance and knowledge that we are secure in Christ's love and our present life is but a journey of faith until we get to heaven.

For my youth group teenagers, I try to promote this important teaching: **In their lives, the STM trip is just one part of the journey.** When we return home from a mission trip, we are in one sense going home, and it is wonderful to see our parents and friends again (and get connected back to technology). Yet, I want them to know that the journey of life and faith continues because we have not reached our final destination yet. The teaching gives our youth the perspective that faith and life continue long after any mission trip ends.

In relation to our two teachings for our youth group, I would strongly mandate at least two follow-up meetings for any STM trip. Our youth group does three. (Section V's guide to the Interactive Journal also contains three.) The purpose of these meetings would not just be to reiterate the continuing journey of faith and missions throughout all of life. These meeting would serve two other purposes as well. First, these meetings let teens and adults share and convey post-mission-trip struggles, an act that can be spiritually therapeutic and encouraging to others who are also struggling. Second, you can use these meetings to help teenagers not live in the past.

Of course, we can share the glories and wonderful work that God has done during the mission trip and through each person as a way to affirm the power and presence of God. But we can also promote the hope for each of our youth, as Hebrews 13:8 says, that the same Jesus is with them, yesterday, today, and forever, as well as before, during, and long after the STM trip.

Finally, as far as follow-up times, our youth group also has a time of evaluation after the mission trip—for both the teens and leaders. My most tenured ministry intern Josh, who I noted earlier packaged the "mottos" for me, came up with this evaluation template after years of our group asking the same evaluation questions. I have seen its usefulness to help our teens and adult leaders concretely reflect on our past mission trip, so that our future mission trips could benefit.

It is a simple yet open-ended evaluation process. I love it because it allows each person to think individually about the mission team and all that has happened. It invites thinking from different angles, but it's also a deeper spiritual process that provides follow-up for your teens and adults, helping them look back *and* move forward. Josh has traveled extensively with our group on domestic and international mission trips, which helped him created this. We call this tool the "3-2-1 Mission Trip Takeoff Evaluation" (or "3-2-1 Evaluation," for short). I like it because it not only helps individuals evaluate what our past trip has been like, it also serves as a countdown to their future life and growth after the STM trip. I've included the actual tool, as well as a leader's guide, which expounds on the reasoning behind each question. (You can see how I suggest utilizing the 3-2-1 Evaluation on page 311 of Section V.)

3-2-1 MISSION TRIP TAKEOFF EVALUATION TOOL

3 - Share 3 things that really blessed you on the mission trip.
- This is meant to remind us about the goodness of God and how every good and perfect gift is from above (James 1:17), so that we can share in God's goodness together.

2 - Share 2 things that you've learned from this trip—whether from pastors, teachers, or your peers, or from what you experienced on the mission trip.
- How can these specific things that you've learned as a man/woman benefit you in Kingdom work in the future?

1 - Share 1 thing that you think you, yourself, could improve, change, or do differently as you move forward.
- How has this mission trip challenged you to grow as a as a man/woman of God?

3-2-1 MISSION TRIP TAKEOFF: EVALUATION TOOL

Leader's Guide

3 - Share 3 things that really blessed you on the mission trip.
- This is meant to remind us about the goodness of God and how every good and perfect gift is from above (James 1:17), so that we can share in God's goodness together.

Leader's Notes
In this "3" section, we focus on celebrating what God has done on the trip or in the lives of each individual. This is not time for critiques and complaints from our adult leaders and teenagers. We use the first part of the evaluation to celebrate what God has done. The open-ended nature of this part of the evaluation enables each person to think to think about their lives and what happened on the trip, as well as encounters with people they met or experiences with God. We often see teens and adults talk about their life-changing moments, as well as how they saw God working in the mission field or in the lives of someone they met. We can value this time and it is always a wonderful celebration of all the work God has done.

2 - Share 2 things that you've learned from this trip—whether from pastors, teachers, or peers, or from what you experienced on the mission trip.
- How can these specific things that you've learned as a man/woman benefit you in Kingdom work?

Leader's Notes
While this part of the evaluation may have some overlap with the first part, it is meant to zero in on what each person has learned and have a "forward" focus. We hope that by naming their teach-able moments, these moments can impact their future as well. Sometimes, we see youth name or express a limitation they realized during this part of the evaluation. Other times, they might express a realization of how God can use an individual for his purposes. It might even be a Bible verse that became more real and evident amidst the everyday work on the mission field. In reflecting on what

we have learned, we also reflect on how it has taught us something to take into our future.

1 - Share 1 thing that you think you, yourself, could improve, change, or do differently.
- How has this mission trip challenged you to grow as a man/woman of God?

Leader's Notes
We frame this last part of the evaluation within the context of "you" because it is meant to provide feedback, critique, change, areas of improvement, or things or ways we, as individuals, can do things differently. In framing it within the context of "you," the person is reflecting on how THEY need to change or improve. As people share these things with each other in this context, there is no doubt that more areas for improvement and change will become evident. Moreover, it is a good gateway to frame the question of more general areas for critique, improvement, or change for future trips or any kind of service to God. However, because it BEGINS with self-reflection, the tendency is that unlike more general critique and reflection, people CAN focus inwardly as team members, rather than pointing the finger at someone else.

POSTSCRIPT | TO THERE AND BACK AGAIN

Whenever I think of STM trips and my 44 trips—19 overseas—I keep wanting to compare each one to the *Lord of the Rings* and *Hobbit* movies. Perhaps it sounds overly dramatic and cliché to do so. Our mission trips were not adventures where we faced Orcs or the Nazgûl chased us down. But in other ways, they were quite fantastic adventures and journeys, where we ventured near and far to do good.

My favorite of all the *Lord of the Rings* movies is still the first one: *The Fellowship of the Ring*. The mission to destroy the ring was birthed. The group faced a lot of struggles along the way and, in the end, what some people disliked was that the first movie ended so suddenly. People left the movie theater wanting more, because it seemed like the movie was just beginning in many senses. You had to leave without knowing what would come next.

Perhaps an STM trip is sort of like that. Or at times it has felt like that. It just ends, and you don't know what is going to happen next. It was a great adventure, a great trip, your group overcame many things and trials, and then it just seems to end. To combat this idea of just ending, I have proposed and endorsed an STM philosophy that is more preparation and discipleship based. STMs must be so incorporated in the daily and year-round life of the youth ministry and church, that missions and even STMs becomes less of an event or "trip" during the summer. STMs must be part of any youth ministry's long-term teaching and practice about missions and the church. It must be part of the youth group before, during, and after the STM trip. It cannot just end at the point of coming home or even as the summer turns to fall and the academic year causes teens' STM trip memories to do a slow fade.

However, while we can (and need to) not let this happen, there is still the reality that the STM trip does end and we don't know what is going to happen next. Even if you had read all the *Lord of the Rings* books before seeing the first movie, there was still something unsatisfying about the movie just ending and having to wait for the sequels.

MISSION TRIPPING

I think that STMs with youth groups and teenagers and youth ministry in general is just like watching the first *Lord of the Rings* movie when you haven't seen the others yet. We don't know what will happen next after the mission trip ends, and we don't know what the next parts will be. The *Lord of the Rings* trilogy eventually ended with a happy ending and evil was destroyed. Today, many years later, I have seen all three parts of the trilogy and feel a satisfaction when I think about the three movies as a whole, even when I just watch parts of the first movie over and over when it comes on television. Viewing all three movies, we can see what the ultimate journey was for and how it ended in such a powerful and hopeful way.

So, I want to encourage those youth workers, volunteers, adult leaders, and others taking these short-term missions journeys—the real ultimate journeys—with their teens. At my church, I have tried to do everything I have written about in this book, especially trying to turn a short-term missions trip into a long-term (and even daily) lifestyle for teens. Missions is part of our youth group ministry before, during, and long after our trip. However, following each trip, I am still not sure of what will happen next. It is in that sense that any one STM trip is just "part one" in the lives of our teenagers. It is powerful and hopeful, but not yet our "ending."

While there are many critiques of STM trips, I still believe with all my heart, soul, mind, and strength that they are one of the most important things you can do in youth ministry. I say this because I know God is good, and he changes the hearts of our STM trip team and the people we will meet, minster to, and partner with on the mission field. Philippians 1:6 says, "And I am sure of this, that he who began a good work in you will bring it to completion at the day of Jesus Christ" (ESV). God is the Author and Perfector of our hearts, our youth, and our STM trips. He is faithful. And in the end, somehow the ring was cast into the fire and all the goodness of Middle Earth was restored. Likewise, I know that through our STM trips with our youth groups, the goodness of God is being restored.

SECTION V
15 MEETINGS: BEFORE, DURING, & AFTER YOUR TRIP

INTRODUCTION
Using *Mission Tripping: An Interactive Journal*
(Leader's Guide)

In this final section of the book, we'll explore **Mission Tripping: An Interactive Journal, the 15-part workbook and meeting guide** to help you and your team prepare for and successfully navigate an STM trip. The first six parts are for meetings before you leave, the second six parts are for meetings while you are on the mission field, and the final three parts are for meetings after you return. There is great flexibility in this preparation guide, and you can use all the lessons, some of the lessons, or combine them. Moreover, how you use the guide will depend on your meeting schedule and time parameters before, during, and after the trip. You may even have additional meetings.

The guide is based on sections two through four of the book. It's meant to complement the material in those sections, and you can refer back to those sections of the book as needed. *Mission Tripping: An Interactive Journal* is meant to be easy for your teens to use, includes material from the book, and includes space for answers to questions, notes, and (of course) journaling. There are also preparation assignments for the youth to tackle between meetings. It's very flexible by design, to promote discussion or times of personal reflection where teens can write down their answers first and *then* discuss them. You can use it in smaller group formats or as an entire team together. Or you can vary that from meeting to meeting, or section to section. Finally, it's something they can use for the duration of the mission trip—for preparation before you go, spiritual growth during the trip, and continued discussion after you return.

The Leader's Guide provided here includes everything from the youth journal as well as details and suggestions specifically for leaders. Each meeting contains an introduction to be read at home (or together before each meeting, if you choose) and a space for your youth to journal their thoughts. **(More space for this journaling is provided in the youth version than here in the Leader's Guide.)** After that, the actual meeting is broken down into five sections and contains details and suggestions for you as you prepare your youth and work through the meetings. (You'll find these details under the aptly titled "Leader's Notes.")

The five sections of each meeting break down as follows:

 **SHARE**

During the first section or time period of each meeting, you as the leader are invited to share prayer topics and then spend time in opening prayer with your mission team—both adult leaders and youth. Additionally, use this time to share with your team any administrative details regarding the trip, such as future meeting schedules, packing lists, etc. Finally, this section will always have some sort of ice-breaker or discussion starter to set up the focus of that particular meeting.

 **AWARE**

The second section of each meeting is a transition from the opening/ice-breaker to the element of the STM trip you want to focus on for that week.

 DARE

In this section of each meeting, you'll dig deeper with your youth into the focus of the meeting. It will involve Scripture and deeper theology but will also use elements of whole-group discussion, small-group discussion, and teaching.

PREPARE

Toward the end of each meeting, the focus will be specifically on preparing your team. This means reminding them again of any administrative details of the mission trip you went over in the SHARE time, preparing them for the next meeting times, and introducing and giving them any "homework" or assignments they need to prepare before the next meeting.

PRAYER

After PREPARE is done, the last part of the meeting is devoted to prayer. There will be different ways to close out the meetings each week in a prayer exercise, varying from personal or group reflection/prayer, simple sharing of prayer topics, some final Scriptures to reflect on, etc., but ultimately all of these formats culminate in a specific time devoted to prayer itself.

I would emphasize that each of these five parts—SHARE, AWARE, DARE, PREPARE, and PRAYER—offers flexibility and room to be creative and also to work within your individual time parameters. I understand that parents are bringing their teenagers to meetings and waiting to take them home. Hence, I value a youth leader's individual sensibilities and believe in giving you as adult leaders some freedom and flexibility for each meeting.

ANTICIPATION: GOING THERE

ACT I | MEETINGS 1-6

1: VACATION VS. MISSION

Leader's Notes
For each scheduled meeting, your group will have a personal introductory reading meant to be done on their own at home, as well as space for journaling. (You might choose to accomplish the pre-meeting reading and journaling together, however, if that works for your group and timeframe.)

Personal Reading
What is the most exciting day of the week for you? Mondays? Probably not. Maybe for you, it's Fridays? After all, it's the last day of the school week, you probably get some time to relax Friday night, and at the very least, you don't have school the next day. There is definitely a difference between a Monday morning and a Friday morning for you as a teenager, with the daily grind of school.

In the same way that there is a difference between a Monday and a Friday, we want to start thinking about the difference between a mission trip and a vacation. We all need times to rest and relax, and vacations can provide that time. Some people like to equate vacations with the idea of "Sabbath" rest in the Bible. Perhaps your family is used to taking vacations yearly or going on other trips to relax.

Going on a short-term mission is a trip, yes. But it's a very different type of trip. Sure, it can be fun, and mission trips should involve great elements of joy and fellowship. But it also involves so many other things.

My thoughts, feelings, fears, and joys right now...

[More space provided in Interactive Journal.]

Leader's Notes
This first meeting is the first official STM preparation meeting for your youth and adult leaders. At this point, your team should be set, and teens should be committed to your STM trip. However, as the leader of your team, when/how you choose to have your youth make that commitment is your call. It can be a financial deposit, a team-individual or leader-individual covenant of some kind, or a combination. Regardless, it's best to head into the first meeting having firm commitments from your team.

Pray: *Always open with a word of prayer, to set the right tone that this is a mission trip, not just any service or social justice activity.*

Review: *Review any meeting schedule and remind the team about any commitments/expectations you have for them. I usually have a parent-youth covenant form with expectations for meeting attendance and preparation, along with dates and times for all meetings. I also permit the youth two excused absences. On a side note, after a teen misses two meetings, I meet with the individual parents and the youth and discuss the attendance policy and remind them that they are in jeopardy of not being able to go.*

Additionally, review any other administrative aspects of the trip that you feel are important. Perhaps fundraising expectations and goals would be a good issue to discuss, as it is early in the STM trip preparation and teens need to be aware of this important part of the trip.

MEETING #1

 **SHARE**

Things We Need to Prepare For

1.

2.

3.

4.

5.

Thoughts and Reflections

1. Think and share about the best vacation you have ever taken. If you have not taken any memorable vacations, perhaps you can share about a fun trip or experience you have had with you family recently.

2. Why were these vacations or trips so enjoyable and fun? Jot down some thoughts below.

3. What are your expectations of the trip and thoughts about the trip? Do you think it will be hard or difficult? What are you looking forward to? What are you not looking forward to?

4. How do you think a mission trip is different from a vacation? In what ways can they overlap?

5. Why are you going on the mission trip?

 **AWARE**

Leader's Notes

Using the table from chapter 11, outline and highlight some of the differences between a mission trip and a vacation. After you highlight the differences with your youth by going over the table, go through the following questions. You will need to help your group fill in the blanks in their journal with the words in bold here.

VACATION	MISSION TRIP
1. Serve __**self**__	1. Serve ____**others**____
2. __**Inward**__ Focus	2. __**Outward**____ Focus
3. Paying to have ____**fun**____ (Although you will have fun)	3. Paying (fundraising) to ____**hard work**____
4. Paying to be ____**served**__	4. Fundraising to ____**serve**____
5. The cost of __**enjoying self**__	5. Cost of ____**sacrifice**____
6. ____**Fee**____ Shows you want to go	6. __**Dedication**__ Shows you want to go
7. Fee ____**reserves**____ your spot.	7. Dedication and commitment ____**reserve**____ your spot.
8. Little or no ____**work**____	8. Hard __**work**__, __**homework**__, heart __**work**__
9. ____**Fun**____ for me	9. __**Heart**__ of me
10. Unity = __**Togetherness**__	10. Unity = United with/in __**Christ & his purpose**__
11. ____**No**____ Cares about life	11. __**Cares**__ About life in Christ and others
12. No cares about our __**actions**__	12. Words and action __**either display**__ Christ or Opposite
13. __**Once**__ a Summer	13. Long __**before**__ and __**after**____ the Summer

1. As you look at the table, circle three points that you need to be reminded of and remember the most. Take some time to share with the group the three you circled and why they are personally so important for you to remember.

2. What else would you add to the list in the table? What do you need some clarification about? What don't you agree with?

 **DARE**

Leader's Notes
You can do this in smaller groups or as one large mission team in a circle. It's a great idea to get the other adult leaders involved at this stage as well by perhaps breaking up into smaller groups and having them each lead a group or having them participate with the teens in some other way. The ultimate goal is for adults (and your youth) to all feel part of the group and bond. (After all, it needs to start sometime.)

1. So, how can we begin to think about missions and our STM (Short Term Missions) trip from a biblical perspective? Read Matthew 28:16-20.

2. Matthew 28:16-20 may be the most quoted verses in the Bible when it comes to missions. Notice verse 19 and the word *go.* What does that word imply?

Leader's Notes
You can discuss with your youth the idea of "commission" from chapter one.

3. Consider verses 16 and 17. What do you notice about the disciples as they gathered? What were they feeling and thinking as Jesus sent them to "go"? In what ways is this encouraging or discouraging to you?

Leader's Notes
The goal of this question is to get your team to consider the disciples. We know disciple *means "follower of Christ," but they were not "Super Christians." They were tax collectors and fisherman. In other words, ordinary, common men. In fact, right before Jesus commissioned them for his mission work, Matthew 28:17 says, "And when they saw him they worshiped him, but some* **doubted***." In other words, it shows that these disciples were not perfect, were filled with doubt, were unsure as they were sent to go. This should give teens hope as they consider what missions is all about. It is a call to go and is a commission for ordinary people, just like them.*

4. Next, read verses 18 and 19. Although some of the disciples were doubting at this time, what can we notice from these verses that can encourage you?

Leader's Notes
Your teens may have various thoughts and feelings about being part of an STM team, including doubt—just like the disciples. The question was asked earlier in the meeting, "Why are you going on the short-term mission trip?" Some teens may be going because they want to do community service. Others may be going because their parents have encouraged them to go on the STM trip. Whatever their situation, we want teens to notice that Jesus is sending his disciples with all authority in heaven and on earth.

5. Consider the following quote from theologian Phillip Bethancourt as you think about Matthew 28:16-20, especially verses 18 and 19:

"In the great commission, King Jesus issues his discipleship battle plan to the church because he possesses 'all authority in heaven and on earth' (Matthew 28:18). Jesus sends his soldiers to the front lines to engage the kingdom of darkness."

Phillip Bethancourt

Phillip Bethancourt, "10 Connections Between Jesus and the Kingdom of God," The Gospel Coalition (online), February 24, 2014, http://www. thegospelcoalition.org/article/10-connections-between-jesus-and-the-kingdom-of-god

How do this quote and verse 18 impact your rationale for going on a mission trip? How might these truths make a difference if you are doubting your participation in the STM trip?

6. Remember: Missions is a **commission** for ordinary people—but a commission with the **authority** and **power** of Jesus.

Leader's Notes
The youth guide does not contain the answers given above for you in bold. You will need to work through the answers with your group.

 **PREPARE**

Do some research and reflection at home this week:
1. Spend time researching your STM location. Find out about the community, local demographics, and what kind of needs there are in that community. Write down and come prepared to share three facts about the community you will be visiting and three needs of that community.

Three facts:

1.

2.

3.

Three needs:

1.

2.

3.

2. Read Acts 1:8 and think about the different locations that were mentioned for "missions" in this verse. Reflect and write down your thoughts on why there were different locations that the church was called to be "witnesses" to.

3. Reflect on and jot down whatever was most impactful from today's meeting for you.

Leader's Notes
Close this week's meeting by having each teen share personal prayer topics related to the trip, and then, as a leader, share any other team prayer requests that you would want them to pray about during the week. (For example, request prayer for each team member, for the people you will meet and location you will be going to, for traveling mercies on the trip, etc.) As indicated, offer a time for suggestions from the team for other prayer topics. Then spend time praying as a group.

PRAYER

- What is your biggest reservation/fear/concern about the STM trip and what are you looking forward to the most? Share with others. Jot down names and prayer requests here to pray for during the week.

- What are some other team prayer requests that our team can pray about during the week?

Spend some time in prayer right now.

Dear Jesus...

2: WHERE ARE WE GOING? THIS TRIP AND BEYOND

Personal Reading

Have you ever had a surprise party thrown for you? It is a joyful, also *surreal* feeling in those first few moments when everyone yells "surprise!" You are disoriented, looking around to see all the people there and probably thrilled but also a little lost in the moment.

And you might be too young to go on blind dates, but you probably know what they are. They are, of course, when people try to set you up with another person you've never met. It's an odd feeling, and it can get awkward trying to get to know them in a few minutes.

When you arrive on the mission field, you don't want it to be like a surprise party or a blind date. It will be a great "surprise" going on any mission trip, being in a new location, and meeting new people. But trying to get to know the location after you arrive can be as awkward as a blind date, and it can cause the mission trip to get off to a rocky start.

My thoughts, feelings, fears, and joys right now...

MEETING #2

 **SHARE**

Leader's Notes
Pray: *Always open with a word of prayer.*

Share: *This second meeting is a great time to have teens open up and share about their thoughts and reflections from their "homework" as well as reflections from their personal prayer requests at the previous meeting.*

Review: *Review any final thoughts about the differences between a vacation versus a mission trip as well as thoughts from Matthew 28:16-20. Give time for questions from the week before as far as things the team needs to prepare for or any of the administrative things you went over.*

Quickly review and re-emphasize with the team things they need to be reminded of as far as preparation. Consider forms you need to collect. While it is early in the process, hopefully, beginning to go over personal packing lists for your team is a good idea at this meeting or sooner, rather than later. Teenagers may pack at the last minute, but some parents may want to begin preparing sooner.

What You Need: *This meeting's opening activity deals with understanding a location and finding details about a location using food and restaurants as an example. Your teens will need access to their smartphones in order for this to work.*

Thoughts from Last Week and Things We Need to Prepare For:

1.

2.

3.

4.

5.

Thoughts and Reflections

1. What is your favorite restaurant or place to eat around your area? Why?

2. Pair up into groups and take out your cell phones. Each pair will be assigned a major city in the United States for this activity.

> **Leader's Notes**
> *Assign each group a random but major US city like New York, San Francisco, etc.—as long as it's not the city you live in.*

3. Imagine you are going to visit your assigned city on a food tour. What restaurants would you like to visit and why? Use your phones to research three restaurants you would like to eat at in your assigned city.

After a few minutes, share with the other groups about your findings.

4. Why could it be important to know about a location before you get there?

> **Leader's Notes**
> *After giving the groups some time to research and share with the others, they will naturally come to the*

conclusion this question suggests, that if they were going to visit a city on a food tour, they would want to do research about the best places to eat or their experience might be totally altered for the worse. Similarly, if we are going to a location to do an STM trip, we would want to do research about the location ahead of time to do the best mission work we could.

 **AWARE**

Leader's Notes

In the previous meeting's "homework," your team was asked to find out about the community, local demographics, and what kind of needs there were in the area of their STM location. Now is when that information will be shared with others.

You can make this activity fun by making it competitive, tallying points for new information, giving out candies to those who share, etc. You might even give a prize to the individual who has the most unique answer or answers.
Note: *Some of your youth may have not prepared or done anything outside of the group after the first meeting. I would strongly discourage publicly calling out any individual teens the first time it happens. However, if you can speak to the team as a whole in more general terms, this is a good time to stress the importance of personal—as in using their own time—preparation for the STM trip, as well as how it is a reflection of each person's commitment to the trip.*

In this exercise you may find that your teens repeat many of the same answers, especially because they all probably used Google and Wikipedia to find the same information. Come prepared as a leader to offer deeper information than what a cursory internet search can offer. If traveling overseas, Operation World will be a great resource. If traveling within the US, most communities have local town or even county information online.

Throughout this section, emphasize the importance of knowing where they are going to be serving and why they are going to that location by pointing out how this information impacts your trip and preparation for the trip (e.g., "there are high numbers of Hindus in this community, which means we ought to have at least a basic understanding of Hinduism in order to communicate what sets the gospel of Jesus apart from Hinduism").

1. Share your research on the team's STM trip location.

2. As you listen to others, write down a few things you learned from another team member that you did not know but was interesting to you.

3. In sharing details about your location for your STM trip, why do you think it is important to know about your location? You talked about this a few minutes ago, but now that you have heard from each other about your location, think about it again.

4. What difference can it make for this mission trip?

Leader's Notes
Push your team to find the connections between key information and its potential relevance to your trip on their own as much as possible, but guide with prompts when needed. (Think: weather impacts clothes to pack, local food impacts nutritional expectations, cultural demographic may impact what is appropriate behavior, etc.)

 **DARE**

1. Read Acts 1:8. What are some of the reflections you had from last week on this passage?

2. What can we learn about missions based on the different distances that were needed to travel for mission work? Was it *just* about the different distances needed to travel? What was the significance of the Samaritans mentioned in this verse?

Leader's Notes

As explored in chapter one of the book, this verse seemingly connotes the varying "travel" and "distance" aspects of missions. In considering this verse, we can see that there are multiple locations mentioned for a reason. There was a call for missions to Jerusalem, which shows missions can be more local. There were missions to Judea and Samaria, which required more travel, perhaps about a day or so. Finally, there was call to go to the "ends of the earth," which you can imagine, could be a much longer mission trip.

However, not only is the variety of distances/times something noteworthy from this verse, but for New Testament believers in the early church, it was evident and probably shocking to see the Samaritans mentioned in this call for missions. Samaritans were outcasts from the Jewish culture, but there was a calling to go to the Samaritans as a mission field and not merely their local Jerusalem community. Hence, God has called his people to even the most rejected of the culture and times.

This understanding of missions will benefit our youth as we can nurture in them a theology of missions that

*is not just an event they do in the summer. There
are a variety of distances and variety of people God
has called Christians to go to and be witnesses to.
Missions is the calling of the church and the teens'
lives short term and long after the trip, for a variety of
communities and people.*

3. As we think about the last point, we also want to consider it in terms of what church is. Where is your church located? What do you like most about your church?

Leader's Notes
*For these questions, most teens will give your church
address or street name as its location. Likewise, when you
ask them what they like about your church, they will say
things like their friends, the youth group (yes!), or perhaps
church activities. That's okay. We'll get to a bigger picture
of church…*

5. There is a deeper meaning to the idea of *church*. Read Matthew 12:30.

a. The word *church*, in the original Greek language, is based on the idea of "__**gathering**__."
b. The __**ultimate**__ mission of God, in Jesus Christ, is to gather his people.
c. __**God**__ is the great and original missionary.
d. "Gathering" is the fundamental and greatest __**priority**__ of God and his church.
e. By definition then, church __**IS**__ missions, as it (the church) is "gathered" together by Christ and then called to "__**gather**__" others.

Leader's Notes
*The youth journal does not contain the answers given
above for you in bold. You will need to work through*

the answers with your group.

As discussed in chapter one, the word **church***, in the original Greek language, is based on the idea of "gathering." This "gathering" function of the church has many aspects. For example, it means to gather as a Body of Christ and gather as his people. However, it also describes the ultimate mission of God, in Jesus Christ: to gather his people. God is the great and original missionary. Jesus came to "gather" and call his people to "gather" others. Ultimately, as Matthew 12:30 says, "Whoever is not with me is against me, and whoever does not gather with me scatters." Hence, "gathering" is fundamental and of the greatest priority to God's church. Church is a gathering of God's people and a subsequent call for all his people to be gatherers with Jesus and share about Jesus with others, so that others would then "gather." This is vital to teach our youth, because to understand church is to understand missions. The church is not only the meeting place of the youth group and the "starting" point of their mission trip, but by definition, the church IS missions, as it is "gathered" together by Christ and then called to "gather" others.*

Last week in our mission trip vs. vacation chart, the last point was that vacations may be **once** a summer, but missions is something to be done **long before** and **after** the summer. We all need to understand how our church and missions are one in the same.

6. Brainstorm together specific ways the youth group can do missions as more than just going to a location this summer, but as a practice that continues long after the summer. List some ideas below.

Leader's Notes
Our church does a "mission" activity each season

*to help promote this—something that perhaps can
be initiated in your youth group. This will take some
research for you and hopefully the youth as well. We
do 30-Hour Famine in late winter, an Easter outreach
as spring ends, summer missions in the summer
(obviously), and a fall outreach to children.*

 **PREPARE**

Do some research and reflection at home this week:
1. Think about what makes a good missionary, in your opinion.
List five things.

1.

2.

3.

4.

5.

2. Use the internet and research common criticisms of STM
trips. Or, you can also do research on what makes a "bad"
mission trip. List five potential issues based on that research.

1.

2.

3.

4.

5.

Leader's Notes
*Most teens won't be surprised that non-Christians are
critical of short-term missions trips, but some may be
jolted by the reality that some Christians also criticize
them. Reassure them that you'll be working through
the criticisms together later and advise them not*

be discouraged by what they read—you'll seek the
solutions as a team at the next meeting.

3. Take time this week to think about ways the youth group can do missions, not just during the STM trip time, but year round.

PRAYER

- Spend time praying for your local community that you are going to be visiting and serving.

- Spend time praying for a bigger "heart" for missions for each person on the team and your church and youth group.

Dear Jesus...

3: READY? OR NOT? (AND HOW TO BE)

Personal Reading

A famous actor once discussed how every time he was put on stage or in front of a camera, he would get nervous and have self-doubt about his performance. He never felt quite comfortable acting in front of an audience or the camera. However, he noted that in spite of all his doubts he lived by these words: "the humility to prepare, and the confidence to pull it off." This gave him all the strength to be an effective actor despite his self-doubts. He had diligently prepared for his acting roles, with humility, which gave him the confidence to pull it off.

As you prepare for your mission trip, weekly assignments are not just things that your leader wants you to do to keep you busy. But they *are* a sign of humility, that you can embrace the importance of your mission trip and diligently prepare. Moreover, as you do, you can have more confidence—not just in yourself but that God is going to use you during this mission trip and beyond.

My thoughts, feelings, fears, and joys right now...

MEETING #3

 **SHARE**

Leader's Notes
Pray: *Always open with a word of prayer.*

Share: *This third meeting is a good time to have your team assess their preparation so far for the mission trip. Ask them what they have found helpful and what they are struggling with as they prepare.*

Review: *This is a good time to check up on any fundraising efforts that teens are doing, either individually or as a group. Be sure to give updates on how fundraising goals are being met.*

Encourage the team at this time to continue in their diligent preparation for the trip. Especially with "homework" and prayer between meetings

What You Need: *Get a hold of Anthony Bourdain's video where he eats "anus" ("No Reservations" Season 3, Episode 4, Namibia) or the first few minutes of his Piers Morgan interview (link to interview below). Take a few minutes to watch one or both clips.*

Link: http://www.huffingtonpost.com/2012/11/14/anthony-bourdain_n_2129102.html

Things We Need to Prepare For

1.

2.

3.

4.

5.

Thoughts and Reflections

1. What is the most disgusting thing you have ever eaten? Describe it and why it was so disgusting.

2. Have you ever eaten anything gross that one of your parents or perhaps another family member made for you, and they were sitting right next to you when you tasted it? What did you do? How did you respond?

3. What can we learn from Anthony Bourdain about reacting to "disgusting" foods that are served to us by others? Why do you think he responds the way he does? Why it is important?

 **AWARE**

Leader's Notes

Today's meeting will focus on getting ready for a mission trip and, in particular, going to new locations that may be different than what your youth (and even adult leaders) are used to. How they respond in these local contexts can make the trip a successful one or a not successful one. The video and prior questions were focused on how responding negatively to someone giving you certain foods would be disrespectful and harm your relationships with them, but now it's time to dig deeper into the importance of thoughtfulness in general in regard to the trip—namely thoughtfulness and purposefulness with each STM trip decision, not just our behavior.

During this section, you'll be making time to review and discuss their "homework" from the week before. You'll want to focus on ways we can be the best short-term missionaries. The assignment asked them to:
    a. Go home and research what makes a good missionary—in their opinion.
    b. Research criticism of STM trips or what makes a mission trip "bad."

They should have a list of five issues to discuss.

After seeing how sensitive Anthony Bourdain was to his hosts when it came to food, we want to consider how we can be sensitive and *effective* missionaries as we visit new and different places than we are used to.

1. First, take a few minutes to review from last week ways your youth group can do missions not just during the STM trip time but year round. What did you come up with? Write down two thoughts you hear from other people on your team that you really like.

    1.

    2.

2. From our list you made during the week, what makes a good missionary in your opinion? Write down two thoughts you hear from other people on your team (that you did not list) that you think are important.

    1.

    2.

3. From the list you made during the week, what are some major criticisms of STM trips or—in other words—what makes

a "bad" mission trip? Write down two thoughts you hear from other people on your team (that you did not list) that you think are important.

1.

2.

 **DARE**

1. Read 2 Corinthians 6:3. What do you think it means to be an "obstacle" (ESV) or "stumbling block" (NIV) for another person?

2. Connect the idea of being an obstacle with the notion in that verse that "no fault may be found with our ministry." Or, depending on your translation, "no one can discredit your ministry." Why are the two ideas connected? What would this mean for you as a missionary going to a location where you will be meeting new people?

Leader's Notes
Teenagers will encounter new and challenging situations when they go on a mission trip. It could be encountering a different socio-economic situation, people who are "different" from them (as far as culture goes), living and sleeping conditions they are not used to, etc. You should have already discussed encounters with new and different foods (sometimes even if you are going on a domestic mission trip) in your opening discussion. Ultimately, wherever they go for their mission trip, their actions will speak louder than their words. We want to remind them of the great opportunity to be example to others. In the prayer time at the end of the meeting, 1 Timothy 4:12 will be the focus. But you can introduce it here as well to

encourage them, despite their age, that they can be great examples of Christ.

3. As a missionary during this trip and beyond, we want you to consider three simple things to remember as ways you can move away from being an obstacle to others to being ambassadors and examples of Jesus to others. These three ideas are openness, humility, and teachability. Let's look at each one.

a. Openness:

b. Humility:

c. Teachability:

Leader's Notes
You are welcome to expound on these categories based on your own ideas or based on the ideas I've presented here and in chapter ten. I have used these three simple categories because trying to teach teens all the cross-cultural theories of engagement out there can be quite difficult. Academics often communicate in ways that are dense and not digestible for teens. I have found these categories more tangible. Here is a summary you can share with your group:

a. **Openness:** *Since many of your teenagers may be traveling outside their local area for the first time, try to cultivate a sense of openness. I use the word openness with my teens as a way of conveying to them the need to be open to new ideas, new ways of doing things, and new foods. They do not necessarily have to adopt and embrace everything they encounter. But I teach them that at least being open to them is important.*

b. **Humility:** *It takes humility to be open. I know most teenagers are not necessarily prideful. But it takes humility* to be open. I like the simple definition that Merriam-Webster uses, defining humility as "the quality or state of not thinking you are better than other people: the quality or state of being humble." Teenagers may unknowingly act like they are better than others. But I think that is more their development stage of life. However, they can also be very humble and generous to others, and it's time to encourage that in them.

c. **Teachability:** With openness and humility, youth can also be teachable—in other words, be learners. I try to promote this for our youth. Longer after an STM trip, in our globalized world, they will encounter new things. They are, in fact, probably learning new things every day. In helping them understand and value learning, we are preparing them to open themselves to new things, to seek to understand, and to be able to at least accept differences.

4. Read 1 Corinthians 9:19-23. In light of these verses, consider again the ideas of openness, humility, and teachability. What can the words of the Apostle Paul further teach us about these things? What would you add to what you just reflected on?

 **PREPARE**

Leader's Notes
This week's homework asks each individual to do some reflection about themselves in the context of the mission trip. This will be in tandem with 1 Timothy 4:12, which will be used in the prayer time, but you can also expound on it during this time. We want youth to continue to consider how their lives can and will be an example to others.

Consider these questions at home this week:
1. Do you think your team or you might fail or be a failure on this mission trip? Why or why not?

2. In light of 1 Timothy 4:12, think again about the top three reasons you are going on a mission trip. What are they?

3. How do YOU want to grow and change through this mission trip?

4. How do you want to help OTHER people—and show off God's glory through this trip?

5. What do you expect God to do through you on this trip?

 **PRAYER**

As you close in prayer today, meditate and pray using 1 Timothy 4:12 which says, "Don't let anyone look down on you because you are young, but set an example for the believers in speech, in conduct, in love, in faith, and in purity" (ESV).

- What does this verse say about the amazing opportunity each of you have as young people yourselves? Meditate and pray through the opportunities you each have on this trip.

- Pray for ways that your speech, conduct, love, faith, and purity can set an example for others.

- Pray that your speech, conduct, love, faith, and purity would be something you practice before you leave and when you return home, both individually and as a youth group.

Dear Jesus...

4: LIVING IN LIGHT

We all know God said in Genesis "let there be light," and there was light. But have you ever thought about what that means? Have you ever thought about the importance of light? Maybe you wake up in the middle of the night to go to the bathroom sometimes. Is it completely dark when you venture to the toilet? Is there some crack of light coming from the hallway to make your walk safer to the bathroom? Does your family have nightlights in your rooms, hallways, or bathrooms, so you can see in the middle of the night?

We probably take these kinds of lights for granted. We don't even really think about their importance. However, if we think about it even for a few seconds, we will realize that they provide an extremely important function in our lives. In the same way, as a Christian, you are called to be the light of God. This light can illuminate the love of Christ for those who don't know Jesus. It can even encourage other believers. At the same time, if you don't handle and embrace your role as the light of God, you can also be a "stumbling block" for those you encounter on your mission trip and in your daily life.

My thoughts, feelings, fears, and joys right now...

MEETING #4

 **SHARE**

Leader's Notes
Pray: *Always open with a word of prayer.*

Share: *Review the "homework" from the last meeting time during this opening "share" time and remind teens again of their personal preparation and commitment to the mission team, especially as reflected by doing these assignments at home.*

Review: *Take time to go over any details and paperwork you may need to collect.*

By this fourth meeting, you will perhaps be a few weeks or so from your departure. It is a good idea to go over the personal packing list for each team member again (if you have not already). Please remind teens to take it home to their parents.

Remind your group as you close the SHARE time that the purpose of their homework and reflection from the past week was so that they would be encouraged to not be an obstacle but an example for those they encounter on their mission trip.

Thoughts and Reflections

1. Looking back on your "homework," share what you wrote. Do you think your team or you might fail or be a failure on this mission trip? Why or why not?

2. In light of 1 Timothy 4:12, think again about the top three reasons you are going on a mission trip. What were they?

3. How do YOU want to grow and change through this mission trip? Share what you wrote.

4. How do you want to help OTHER people and show off God's glory through this trip?

5. What do you expect God to do through you on this trip? Talk about that.

 **AWARE**

Leader's Notes
To help illustrate today's time together, have the game Jenga prepared, so your team can play it. Break up the team into two groups that will face off against each other. Have one person from each team come up, one at a time. They will take turns for their team taking off a block and putting it back on top, until one team wins.

You can play a few rounds of this and give some small prizes or incentives to win. For example, the winning team will eat first at the next meal or will be assigned to carry the luggage of the other team during the trip upon arrival. The point of this game is that one block can cause the whole team to lose. This is to illustrate that any person on our team can be a stumbling block that can cause others to be discouraged, either those on our team or those we meet.

What You Will Need: *You'll need to be prepared with a game of Jenga. Depending on the size of your group, you may need a giant or XL Jenga set. These can be purchased readily online.*

1. After you have played, think about the bigger picture of the game dynamic. Are you playing for yourself when you take your turn? What can we learn from playing a simple game like Jenga as teams?

2. How was the whole team affected by one block in this game?

3. Today we are going to be talking about another type of block, a stumbling block. What does it mean to be a stumbling block?

 **DARE**

1. Read 1 John 2:10. This verse connects love, living, and light. How do you see the connection? Why is this important? Jot down some thoughts.

2. This passage also makes the connection that if you love your brother and sister, there is "nothing in them to make them stumble." Think about your personal life and the relationships you have with those around you. This can be school friends, family, or your parents. In what ways can we make others stumble? On the contrary, in what ways can our love encourage others?

3. On our mission trip, our love and lives will either shine the light of Jesus or be a stumbling block for those we meet, if we are not careful. What are ways you can shine the light of Jesus and not be a stumbling block to others? What are ways you risk be a stumbling block to others.

PREPARE

Consider these questions at home this week:

1. Consider our team. What makes a good team member? List three things you would want from a good team member.

1.

2.

3.

2. List three things that you think would make a bad team member.

1.

2.

3.

3. Think about ways your team can be a good witness to those you encounter. We talked about this from an individual perspective already. But how can your team be a good witness to those you encounter and serve with? How can you as individuals affect the team and the team's missionary endeavors?

PRAYER

- Today, form a circle as a team. Go around first and share one way you have been a stumbling block to those in your life and have not been an example of love. Reflect also on how you can change that. After sharing, take some time to pray about these things.

- Next, pray about those you will encounter and meet on the mission trip. It may be local residents in the communities you will visit, local pastors and missionaries, or even random people you will encounter as you travel to your location. Reflect on ways that you can shine the light and love of Jesus with them and not be a stumbling block. Spend some time praying for them.

Dear Jesus...

5: TEAM

Your mission trip this summer is not just about one person. You are going with others. Hence, you are part of a team, a mission team. You can't forget this. You are perhaps used to having a sibling around, a group of friends in school, or classmates at school. But this does not make a team.

What makes you a team is that you and those on your mission team are trying to accomplish a goal together. Each teammate is vital to the success or failure of your team. Any football coach will tell you that the offensive lineman is just as important to the success of a team as the quarterback. Any musical conductor will tell you that the oboe is just as important as the violin.

Teamwork is something you'll need to focus on as you go on the mission trip, as it helps makes the mission trip more effective—not only for your own team but for those your team will encounter. If your team is not getting along or working well together, it will impact your mission team and others you encounter will see it too. You may have heard the saying, "A team is only as strong as its weakest link." Hopefully everyone will be a strong link on a strong team.

My thoughts, feelings, fears, and joys right now...

MEETING #5

 **SHARE**

Leader's Notes:
You are getting down to your last few (two) meetings (unless you planned more) prior to the trip. You should be near completion of your fundraising by now (if not already), and outside of this meeting, you want to make sure you are communicating with parents—not just teens—about the final details of the trip.

Pray: *Always open with a word of prayer.*

Share/Review: *These last few meetings are a good time to talk through issues and procedures for traveling that I outline throughout the book. Expectations for rest stops, van rides, or airport protocol—whichever way you travel— should be discussed now, as well as expectations for electronic items or any other strict packing guidelines. In these latter meetings, so it may stay fresh with the youth, it is important to begin communicating (and reinforcing) these guidelines and expectations.*

Things We Need to Prepare For
1.

2.

3.

4.

5.

Thoughts and Reflections

1. What do you think about this frequently cited acronym: "TEAM = Together Everyone Achieves More!"? How does it relate specifically to a mission team versus a sports team?

2. Alexander the Great famously said: "Remember: Upon the conduct of each depends the fate of all." How might this concept relate to your mission team? Do you think there is some "conduct" of yours that can ruin the "fate" of your mission team?

3. In the assignment after the last meeting, you were asked what make a good team member and what makes a bad team member. Share some of the things you wrote down.

4. How about respect? What does it mean to respect each other? Does it mean you will agree with everything the other person thinks? How does respect relate to your team and team dynamics? What about respecting your team leaders?

 **AWARE**

Leader's Notes

The purpose of this meeting is to think about your team. Not only individually, how each person impacts your team, but how as a team they will be impacting those they encounter and serve on the mission field.

You want to emphasize ways the team as a whole can be a good witness to those you encounter. But, if not careful, they can be a stumbling block as well.

Mottos: *In chapter 10, I outlined mottos that our mission team uses so, as a team, we can be sensitive to those we serve with and serve while on the mission trip. You can take some time to outline them—or come up with your own—and encourage your team to think of more. Note* *that these mottos will be blank in the youth version of the journal, so that your teens can insert the wording and mottos that you choose.*

As discussed in chapter 10, it is much better and easier to say "Motto One" to a teen or your whole team while in the midst of work on the mission field than to stop for a mini-lecture or sermon. Let these function as your team's shorthand for refocusing when behavior, emotions, and motivation falter.

Team Mottos

1. **Leave the place better than you found it.**

2. **Don't hover near another team member. Get involved with those you came to serve.**

3. **If you find yourself idle, do something!**

4. **Love the Lord your God with all your heart, mind, soul, and strength.**

What other mottos do you think could or should be added?

 **DARE**

1. Read Matthew 5:16. What is the connection between our good deeds and others? How can our good deeds impact them?

2. In the same way, how could "bad" deeds impact others?

3. What is the emphasis for our team (and for us as individuals)

from this passage?

**"Remember: upon the conduct of each
depends the fate of all."**

Alexander the Great

Leader's Notes
*Continue to remind the team of the mottos and their
purpose, and that each individual on the team affects the
team and that the team is represented by each individual.
Both the team and individual actions can bring down the
whole team OR, conversely, shine the light of Jesus.*

 **PREPARE**

**Consider this question and tackle these to-dos at home
this week:**
1. What are some additional mottos for your team that you
believe would help shine the light of Jesus to others? Come
to the next meeting with at least two ideas.

1.

2.

2. Take some time this week to look at the packing list with
your parents and assess what you need to purchase and pack.

3. Make sure this week you have the proper luggage for the
trip.

PRAYER

List and share some things you'd like to pray about before you leave.

Leader's Notes
Invite your team to share the prayer concerns they write down.

- Spend some time praying for those you will meet in the mission field.

- Pray for the team, that as a team and individuals you will shine the light of God.

- Pray for your youth group that this trip would be more than just a one-time summer and "short-term" thing.

Dear Jesus...

6: HOW CAN I SERVE?
("SYSTEMIC" MISSIONS)

Personal Reading

When you were in elementary school, did you ever do a class activity where you planted seeds in plastic cups to grow a plant? Do you remember coming to your classroom every day to see its progress? Whether you have or not, no one who has ever planted a seed just sat down next to it, waited patiently for it to grow, and watched it spring up from the ground. In our age of time-lapsed cameras, however, we can see this fascinating phenomenon and watch a plant grow from a seed in a matter of seconds.

You will be going on a mission trip soon, and you will be planting a seed. It may very well grow into a beautiful flower that will be an example of the beauty of Christ. But it will take time. You may or may not be on your mission field long enough to see the flower grow. But that flower, whenever it blooms, will make a difference.

Embark on your mission work during this trip and after it with full confidence that God is using you to grow the seeds of his

Kingdom work.

My thoughts, feelings, fears, and joys right now...

MEETING #6

 **SHARE**

Leader's Notes
While you may have planned for more than six meetings for your mission team, this meeting is written as if it were to be your last meeting before you leave.

Pray: *Always open with a word of prayer.*

Share: *This is the perfect meeting in which to share a little of the team's enthusiasm and excitement with parents and not just the teens. You can invite parents to this last meeting or have a quick short meeting with the parents on the day of your departure. (While you will be busy on the departure day, having a quick meeting then will ensure that most parents are there. Either way, as I suggested in chapter nine, I give parents a detailed schedule of what we will be doing each day of the mission trip so that they can pray for our team. It is a good idea to prepare that also as it can involve parents in the trip, even from afar.*

Review: *Review your meet-up time for departure from the church as well as the return time from your trip.*

Remind teens of any last-minute details, like perhaps the need for spending money during travel days, the need to bring backpacks, or perhaps to bring a lunch on the departure date—whatever their needs will be.

The ministry and spiritual focus in this last meeting will be on having a "systemic" solution perspective on mission service. It should be quite obvious to your team at this point that you are going on a mission trip to serve. As was discussed with teens during previous meetings, and also in the book, there is a lot of criticism out there of STMs. Hence, it is important for your team to have a greater (healthier) perspective of service as they go (and for the rest of their lives).

Things We Need to Prepare For

1.

2.

3.

4.

5.

Thoughts and Reflections

1. How are you feeling about the trip?

2. Do you feel ready to go? Why or why not?

3. What are some last-minute preparations you need to do? Perhaps sharing these can be a helpful reminder to others.

4. Recently, there was a scare at some Chipotle stores with E. coli outbreaks. If you were a Chipotle fan before this, did any of you stop going because of it? Did you tell any of your friends about it or tell them not to go to Chipotle?

Leader's Notes
You'll want to encourage your mission team again that

although an STM trip is by definition "short," God can still use the trip. Moreover, you'll want to encourage them that "missions" is not just a summer thing but is a "lifelong" thing and the lasting impact it has may not be evident during the "short" time they are on the mission field.

5. Some other rumors on social media also insinuated that certain fast food chains were using horse and even rat meat instead of beef for some of their meat products. How would this affect your desire to eat at certain food chains if you knew this were true?

 **AWARE**

Leader's Notes
What You Will Need: *Have a Band-Aid or first-aid kit ready to use as an illustration. (You should have one for the mission trip anyway, so you can use that.) You'll be needing enough Band-Aids to give each teen one prior to starting the discussion portion of the meeting.*

1. If you had a friend with the flu, how would you use this item to help them?

2. What would you try to do to alleviate their flu symptoms?

3. Martin Luther King Jr. once said, "True compassion is more than flinging a coin to a beggar. It comes to see that an edifice which produces beggars needs restructuring." What are your thoughts as you read this quote?

4. How can we apply this quote to our mission trip? How can we apply this to our service projects and anything else our youth group does? How can we view our mission trip and what we are doing while on it, in light of this quote?

 **DARE**

Leader's Notes
Emphasize that God does use each person in vital ways. You can also expound upon Ephesians 2:10 if you want to here.

1. Read 1 Corinthians 3:5-8. What do these verses tell you about your role in the mission field or just more generally in your work and service for God? Is your role important?

2. What do these verses tell you about God's role in his work?

3. If God ultimately makes "the seed grow," how can this encourage you as you go on this mission trip? What is our role and what is God's role in creating lasting change through a mission trip?

4. It is important to remember that perhaps you won't see all the "growing" that God does during this mission trip or during any type of service the youth group will be doing year round. However, how is it encouraging to know God's ultimate role within your work?

Leader's Notes
It is important to emphasize and encourage your teens that God is working to grow the work and service of each of them. There is greater impact from mission trips and service—far greater than we can ever see—because God makes things grow and change over a lifetime, not just days and weeks.

PREPARE

Leader's Notes

Review last-minute reminders. Ask your team to write them down again right here. Emphasize the meeting time at church (or whatever location you are meeting at) for your mission trip departure. Remind them to bring their copies of the Interactive Journal and their Bibles on the trip.

Don't forget any last-minute reminders from your leaders. Write them down here again along with the important details of your departure date, meeting time, and meet-up location.

Departure date: _____

Departure meeting time: _____

Departure meet-up location: _____

**Remember to bring this book
and your Bibles on the mission trip!**

PRAYER

Leader's Notes

If your church has a missions send-off service, that's great. If not, invite some of your church leaders—such as your senior pastor, mission board leaders, or other ministry leaders—to this meeting or this part of the meeting. Have them pray with and for you and your team.

- Pray as a team for safe travels, the health of your mission team, and the people you will be meeting on the mission trip.

Dear Jesus...

ACT II | MEETINGS 7-12

7: FIRST IMPRESSIONS

Personal Reading

We talked about blind dates earlier in this book. When you meet a person for the first time, you may have positive and negative impressions. You have some good vibes about the person, and you may even have some doubts about them. It is amazing, when you hear stories about couples who eventually got married, how many of them had horrible first impressions of the other person.

Your first impressions about your mission field location right now may be positive or negative. You may even have some doubts and may be thinking, "What am I doing here?" and that is okay. Don't let it discourage you. Take some time before the next meeting to share about all your positive and negative feelings about the place you have arrived at. In addition, take some time to find hope and encouragement in your mission team and teammates, as you venture into serving for the rest of your time at your mission trip location.

My thoughts, feelings, fears, and joys right now...

MEETING #7

 **SHARE**

Leader's Notes
Pray: *Always open with a word of prayer.*

Share: *Take some time to assess and see how your team is doing as your travels to your destination are now completed. It is never easy to travel, even short distances. Likewise, carrying and moving personal and team luggage and supplies can be grueling.*

Review: *Keep your team informed of things like bedtimes, wake-up times, and activities/agenda for the next day. Remind your team of the importance of sleep and eating during the mission trip, as discussed in chapter 10, and spend some time getting your group prepared for the days of work and service ahead.*

Note: *In the book, I suggest having evening and morning meetings while you are on the mission field. This is, in part, so that many of your teens can participate in the DARE youth-led devotions (see page 268), but it is also to review and preview each day's work (at your **morning** meetings) and the next day's work (at your **evening** meetings). However, there is only **one** daily meeting guide included here, which is written to be used each evening. You are welcome, though, to use the meeting guide provided in the mornings, split it up between evenings and mornings, or whatever fits your trip and group best. Note that space IS provided in the Interactive Journal for both morning and evening journaling or "reflection."*

Things We Need to Prepare For

1.

2.

3.

4.

5.

Thoughts and Reflections

1. Reflect on all the things that have transpired—from the first day of meetings and preparation, to your travel to the mission trip location, to settling in for the first meeting. How are you feeling about the process? How does God play into your reflections?

2. Spend a few minutes to pray and be grateful for all that has happened up to this point. Pray for and acknowledge the goodness of God.

3. Share your impression of the mission trip so far.

Leader's Notes
If this is your first night, most likely you have not gotten out to work yet, so this time of sharing will be more about the travel, excitement, or something the teens noticed about the location you have come to.

 **AWARE**

Leader's Notes

The DARE portion of the meeting is designed to be youth led starting tomorrow, so now is the time to prepare your team for that. Encourage them that this should not be a stressful or difficult task. They are simply to share a few verses and a few reflections inspired by the verses.

How you set up the rotation is truly going to be dependent on your team size and the number of meetings you'll have. You can ask teens individually or have them sign up (though you may still end up having to ask them directly if you go that route). Take this time to communicate those details as you empower them to take leadership in this way.

Just a note from personal experience that you may want to add to or elaborate on what is said by your youth now and then during the DARE times they lead.

Coming Up: Youth-Led AWARE Times

Starting tomorrow, the DARE time at each meeting will be youth led. This means that one or two of you, either in the morning, in the evening, or both—depending on your schedule—will get to share from the Bible.

When you are assigned or asked to do the DARE time, simply find and read a Bible passage and share some reflections on it with the team. There is no right or wrong way to do this.

 **DARE**

1. Read Luke 10:1-2. Why do you think Jesus sent his servants

out two by two? What does this say to you and the mission team?

2. What does the "two by two" idea say about teamwork? What does it say about accountability?

3. How can you be accountable to others on your team? How do you want them to be accountable to you?

4. Jesus says "the harvest is plentiful" but the "workers are few." What does this say about your important role on the mission trip? What does it say about your mission team?

 **PREPARE**

Leader's Notes
These reflection times are more like journaling and will give teens a chance to write thoughts and feelings down. As I mentioned in previously in chapter 14, it is a good way to keep your team "busy" during down times that mission trips sometimes have. However, this time of reflection or journaling each day can also be used to foster and nurture discussion, so take advantage of it. The youth journal contains plenty of space for your team to do this.

Each evening and each morning, spend time reflecting on the mission trip and writing thoughts and feelings about the prior day. In the evenings, spend time reflecting on the work you have done that day, people you have met, profound experiences, hardships from the day, or any other thoughts you may be having. In the mornings, spend time reflecting again on the past day, but from the perspective of a night's rest (or even unrest). Sometimes a day can seem different or the greater lessons/themes/moments more clear the morning after.

Evening Reflections

Morning Reflections

Reminders for the Team

Leader's Notes
Have you team jot down any important reminders for their day here.

PRAYER

- Reflect on all the things that have transpired from the first day of meetings and preparation, to your travel to the mission trip location, to settling in for the first meeting.

- Share praises to God as you reflect on this, as well as things you have had to overcome to get to this point in your journey.

Dear Jesus...

8: HOW WAS YOUR FIRST DAY?

Personal Reading

Why do Monday mornings going back to school feel so dreary and dreadful? What makes it so hard to go back to school after the weekend? You just finished your first day of serving. There may have been some joys or frustrations. You may have met some new friends and people you are excited about. Or, perhaps the place you are serving is not what you imagined it to be. You may even be feeling tired after your first day or discouraged.

Today, you probably also woke up very early, most likely, to go and serve. So, your body is naturally tired. In fact, you are probably going to get a little more tired each day of your mission trip. That happens to everyone, even teenagers like yourself. The important thing is that you can find the strength and hope to be recharged. The mission trip is a great opportunity (not only for the duration of the trip but long after) to set a great foundation for the rest of your life. It's a way to discover that you can find your hope and strength in God after tough and difficult days. On this mission trip and in life, we will all get tired, we all get weary, and life is not always easy. Find your hope and strength in God.

My thoughts, feelings, fears, and joys right now...

MEETING #8

 **SHARE**

Leader's Notes
Pray: *Always open with a word of prayer.*

Share: *Take some time to assess and see how your team's first day was. Some may have had a great first day. Others may express frustrations or difficulties with the work or food or various other things. This is also a great time to have them share from their reflective journaling the prior evening and that morning.*

Review: *Keep your team informed of things like bedtimes, wake-up times, and activities/agenda for the next day. Remind your team again of the importance of sleep and eating during the mission trip and spend some time getting your group prepared for the days of work and service ahead.*

Things We Need to Prepare For

1.

2.

3.

4.

5.

Thoughts and Reflections

1. What were the most enjoyable parts of serving on your first day?

2. What were the most difficult parts of your first day?

3. Did you make any new friends today? If so, who were they? Share about the person(s) you got to know.

 **AWARE**

1. Read Isaiah 40:28-31. These verses are often quoted for those who are tired, fatigued, or weary. While it is only the first day of the mission trip, you may be more excited rather than tired. However, for some of you, this is the first time you have done this type of work. So, how are you feeling?

2. Notice verse 30 of this passage. It is talking about you, teenagers ("youths"). Perhaps you are not tired after the first day. However, looking back on the past school year, think about and share about a time when you were really tired, fatigued, or weary. What was the cause of it? Was it mental, physical, or even spiritual? How did it make you feel?

3. During your time on this mission trip, you probably will start to feel tired, fatigued, or weary. This is not only a part of this mission trip but a part of life in general. How does this passage encourage us for those times?

4. Do you tend to heed the words of Isaiah 40 in times when you are tired, fatigued, or weary in your life? When have you done so and when have you not? Why?

DARE

Leader's Notes
Have one or two teens share the Scripture and brief reflections they prepared. Be sure to summarize and help make applications based on each of the teen's sharing, if one hasn't already been clear. If time allows, ask the team for thoughts and reflections from their peer's sharing afterward or give them a moment to write something down.

One or two of your peers will share some Scripture and reflections with the group now. Be sure to give them your full attention.

Do you have any other thoughts and reflections from your team member's sharing?

 **PREPARE**

Evening Reflections

Morning Reflections

Reminders for the Team

Leader's Notes
Be sure to prepare your team for anything they need to know for the next day's agenda.

If you weren't able to do so at the beginning of the meeting, take this time to assess how your team are feeling physically after their first day. Many teenagers these days don't do much physical activity or have never done this type of physical activity, so being on a mission trip doing this work may be tough on them. Also, be sure to look out for and remind them about sunburn and wearing sunblock if you are working outside.

PRAYER

Leader's Notes
Take the names of the team members and write them all down on small sheets of scrap paper. Fold them up and put them in a bag or something. Each person will take a folded paper to discover their secret prayer partner for that week.

Today you are going to get assigned one person on the mission team as your prayer partner for the week. Keep this a secret from that person.

MISSION TRIPPING

- Spend the duration of the mission trip praying for your prayer partner, discreetly encouraging them, and supporting them during each work day.

- Pray that you—and your teammates—would be able to trust in the Lord as you get weary, tired, or fatigued this week and in your future.

Dear Jesus...

9: HIS LOVE MADE COMPLETE

Personal Reading

God is love. We hear this all the time. Your probably know it and believe in it to some extent. When you go on a mission trip, you are bound to encounter some people who just overflow with God's love. Although you traveled far to be a witness of God's love to others, although you are excited that your youth group will be a model and example of God's love during this trip and long after this mission trip, although you may be thinking about loved ones back home who love you, you have come on this trip, and you may have met someone so saturated in the love of God, it is contagious.

Is there someone like that you have met? Is there a leader on your trip like that? Is there someone at home like that? Well, truth be told, you are also like that! You are a model and example of God's love. As you continue on this mission trip, and as you and your youth group continue to be "missionaries" long after this mission trip, consider and embrace the truth that God's love is made complete... THROUGH YOU.

My thoughts, feelings, fears, and joys right now...

MEETING #9

 **SHARE**

Leader's Notes
Pray: *Always open with a word of prayer.*

Share: *Take some time again to assess and see how your team and each person is doing. You can ask your team about their reflections and journals during this time.*

Review: *Keep your team informed of things like bedtimes, wake-up times, and activities/agenda for the next day. Hopefully, after today, they will be getting used to the routine and living situation.*

Remind your team again of the importance of sleep and eating during the mission trip and spend some time getting your group prepared for the day of work and service ahead.

Things We Need to Prepare For

1.

2.

3.

4.

5.

Thoughts and Reflections

1. Have you met anyone on this mission trip outside of your team who has been a model of the love of God? Who was it and how have they been an example of God's love?

2. How about on your team? Who has been a model of the love of God? How have they been an example of God's love?

3. Reflect on your life at home. Who has been a model of the love of God? How have they been an example of God's love?

 **AWARE**

1. Read 1 John 4:10-12. (Preferably from the NIV, as these questions are based on the specific wording in that translation.) God loves each of us. The Apostle Paul said in Romans 12 to offer our lives in view of God's mercy (love). Is God's love your motivation for loving others, especially on this mission trip? Why or why not? Is it sometimes hard to love others?

2. Verse 12 is packed with some interesting words. What we want to focus on is that our love for others can be evidence of God's love for others. It is made complete in us in that way also. How can knowing this compel us to love others more diligently?

3. As you have been at your location for a few days, it is a good time to be reminded of your team mottos, as a way of loving those you are meeting, serving, and serving with, during your mission trip. In addition, it's good to reflect on how your love may be made complete through living them out. Review them so you can love others more effectively and God's love can be made complete in you.

Motto 1:

Motto 2:

Motto 3:

Motto 4:

 **DARE**

Leader's Notes
Have one or two teens share the Scripture and brief reflections they prepared. Be sure to summarize and—if it makes sense—help make a practical application after each teen shares, if one hasn't already been clear. If time allows, ask the team for thoughts and reflections from their peer's sharing or give them a moment to write something down.

One or two of your peers will share some Scripture and reflections with the group now. Be sure to give them your full attention.

Do you have any other thoughts and reflections from your team member's sharing?

 **PREPARE**

Leader's Notes
Encourage your team to continue to write about their experiences every night and again in the morning. Encourage them to focus on their actions and the

testimony of their lives. Encourage them to let their lives shine.

Evening Reflections

Morning Reflections

Reminders for the Team

PRAYER

Leader's Notes
Remind your group to be praying for and encouraging the person whose name they chose at the last meeting.

- Pray for people in the community you are serving or serving with.

- Pray for your own team members.

- Pray that the love of God may be complete in you and that your life will be a testament to God's love for others you encounter during this mission trip and when you go home.

MISSION TRIPPING

Dear Jesus...

10: HALFTIME AND BEYOND

Personal Reading
If you like sports movies, you may recollect scenes of great halftime speeches, especially from basketball or football movies. The purpose of these halftime speeches is to assess what has happened in the first half and motivate and inspire what is going to the happen for the rest of the game. A great halftime speech will hopefully help a team finish strong, not only for the present game but for the rest of the season.

Today's session is focused on your halftime. You may be about halfway or a little beyond halfway through your mission trip. We want to discuss things that have been difficult and things that have gone well so far. Perhaps you have made some great new friends (even new friends in your own youth group). Perhaps you have experienced some difficulties that are still nagging at you from during the first half of the mission trip. In doing so, we want to focus on how we can finish well—not only finish this trip but our life after this trip. Perhaps there are relationships at home you need to work on? Perhaps there are things you need to do when you get back? Remember that the mission you have is not just about these "short-term" mission trip days; but that it continues long after the trip.

My thoughts, feelings, fears, and joys right now...

MEETING #10

 **SHARE**

Leader's Notes
Pray: *Always open with a word of prayer.*

Share: *Your group will probably have made it to about the halfway point or a little bit more by now. As the "halftime" of the mission trip, it's a good time to pause and reflect. Invite them to share from their journals at this time.*

Review: *Encourage them in the good they have done and are doing—they need it! And be sure they are prepared for the next day. This can be done at the end of the meeting.*

Things We Need to Prepare For

1.

2.

3.

4.

5.

Thoughts and Reflections
1. What have you enjoyed most about the trip so far? What or who have you fallen in love with?

Leader's Notes
No doubt your team will giggle, thinking of romantic "falling in love," but after a chuckle, remind them our hearts discover love all the time and for many reasons— not just romantic love.

2. What do you miss most about home?

3. Who do you miss from home?

4. Are there any relationships from home you are praying about?

5. What are you looking forward to for the rest of this trip?

6. Don't forget that the mission doesn't end with this trip. It continues for you and the youth group long after this "short" period of time.

 **AWARE**

Leader's Notes
As you go into this time of reading and discussion, say something about it being the halftime of your mission trip and how halftime of any sport is used to rest and reflect on the first half but also to get ready and prepared for the second half.

Read Galatians 6:9 and Philippians 1:6 and divide into two groups. Assign each one either the Galatians verse or the Philippians one. Each group will reflect on the series of questions below for their verse and report back to the other half of group.

1. What does your verse tell you about your work and service

so far and also about the future?

2. How can your verse encourage your group for the rest of the trip?

3. In what ways does your passage impact your service for this trip and beyond, after you go back home?

 **DARE**

Leader's Notes
Have one or two teens share the Scripture and brief reflections they prepared. Be sure to summarize and—if it makes sense—to help make a practical application after each teen shares, if one hasn't already been clear. If time allows, ask the team for thoughts and reflections from their peer's sharing or give them a moment to write something down.

One or two of your peers will share some Scripture and reflections with the group now. Be sure to give them your full attention.

Do you have any other thoughts and reflections from your team member's sharing?

 **PREPARE**

Evening Reflections

Morning Reflections

Reminders for the Team

Leader's Notes
Since it is halftime, don't assume that the focus and motivation of day one is still there. Don't let the little things slip through the cracks with fatigue, instead continue to cover the basics as you prepare for each new day.

**PRAYER**

- Pray for strength not to grow weary in doing good. Pray for hope that the harvest of your mission trip will be fruitful.

- Pray for encouragement and faith that God, who has begun a good work through your mission trip, will see it to completion.

- Pray that the good work God has begun through your mission trip will not just be a summer or "short-term" thing but it will continue in your youth group and each person as you return back home.

Dear Jesus...

11: LOVE HERE, THERE, EVERYWHERE

Personal Reading

Some people are good at meeting new people. They are great at talking with people they've never met and can keep a conversation going for hours. These people seem like they can be best friends with anybody, even after just a few minutes.

It's weird, but sometimes going on a mission trip, you grow in relationships easily and instantly with people you have never met. Or perhaps you have grown in a deeper relationship with someone in your youth group during this trip, who you were not as close with before the trip? Hopefully that relationship will continue and grow deeper when you return.

In addition, if you think about it, there may be people at home you have known for years with whom your relationships do not seem as deep. These relationships may need repairing, even if you have known the friend forever. Maybe it could be a parent or sibling? We want to consider *love* and our relationships back at home as the mission trip ends. God calls us to love one another—and not just here on the mission field. Our love must continue when we get back home.

My thoughts, feelings, fears, and joys right now...

MEETING #11

 **SHARE**

Leader's Notes
This meeting is focused on love again. However, it focuses on the need and call for us to love, not only during this mission trip but when we go home. In my experience, many teens will have a great mission experience where they will experience the love of God—growing closer with the team as well as those they have met during the trip. While the experience of God's love is great during the trip, this meeting also encourages your group to love well when they get back home. It could be their parents, their friends, their siblings. We simply want to challenge them to love those back at home well.

Pray: *Always open with a word of prayer.*

Share: *You can ask your team about their reflections and journals during this time.*

Review: *You may need to get team prepared for going back home at this point or sometime soon. Review travel procedures and go over packing issues.*
Don't forget to go over preparations for the following day.

Things We Need to Prepare For

1.

2.

3.

4.

5.

Thoughts and Reflections

1. What is something that you have fallen in love with about the place you are at? What are some new relationships you have made that you cherish?

2. How will you continue with those relationships, whether you can connect in person with them again or not?

3. While these relationships are great and important, we want to begin to focus on those back home. How can we love those back at home well?

 AWARE

1. Are there relationships here during your mission trip that seem better than certain relationships you have at home? Maybe not as vibrant as the new ones you made this week? Perhaps they are even turbulent and difficult? Describe those relationships.

Leader's Notes

Don't let this discussion question open a gossip session or allow your group to throw out names and situations indiscriminately and without consideration of those not present. But do encourage them to dig deep and look honestly at hurts at home. At the same time, this discussion may open up some deep wounds and hurts, so be prepared for that too.

2. What can you learn from this mission trip, for when you return home?

3. Are there ways you can love those back at home as you have been loving those here?

4. Remember, one of the focuses of our mission trip was that missions is not *just* a short-term idea or practice. What are some communities at home that you can be a missionary to also?

 **DARE**

Leader's Notes
Have one or two teens share the Scripture and brief reflections they prepared. Be sure to summarize and— if it makes sense—help make a practical application after each teen shares, if one hasn't already been clear. If time allows, ask the team for thoughts and reflections from their peer's sharing or give them a moment to write something down.

One or two of your peers will share some Scripture and reflections with the group now. Be sure to give them your full attention.

Do you have any other thoughts and reflections from your team member's sharing?

 **PREPARE**

Evening Reflections

Morning Reflections

Reminders for the Team

Encouragement Notes

With the few days left on our mission trip, we are going to be writing encouragement notes to others. Each person will be given notecards to write a note to each member of the team, as well as anyone on this trip you have served with. (Host church members, people who have fed your team, leaders, or missionaries you have met, etc.) If you are not sure what to write about, reflect on each person and how they have been an encouragement to the team and write to them about that. At the end of the trip, a few people will compile them for each individual person and give them out.

 **PRAYER**

- Pray for the relationships you have made during this trip.

- Pray for the relationships that you will be going home to.

- Think and pray for ways you can rekindle those difficult relationships back at home.

Dear Jesus...

12: PREPARING TO LEAVE

Personal Reading

When you get home, everyone who knew you went on a mission trip will ask, "How was your mission trip?" It's interesting but you will rarely hear anyone answer just flat out that it was horrible. Or, that they hated it and will never return. The natural response will be mostly positive, at the very least. God has probably been revealing himself through this mission trip, and despite any difficulties you may have had, it's probably been a good trip, a positive trip.

Still, you need to prepare to go home. While the mission trip was great, your parents will not let you remain here forever. But what can you take home with you? What can you carry with you, long after you return home? At the next meeting, we'll consider the disciples and what Jesus called them to take with them for the rest of their lives after their mission trip.

My thoughts, feelings, fears, and joys right now...

MEETING #12

 **SHARE**

Leader's Notes
This last meeting will be focused on preparing to go back home, and your team will, no doubt, have various emotions as they anticipate their return to the familiar.

Pray: *Always open with a word of prayer.*

Share: *You can ask your team about their reflections and journals during this time.*

Review: *In the final PREPARE section, there are some things that you need to get your teens equipped for as they get ready to go home. You can begin to discuss them here as well.*

Things We Need to Prepare For
1.

2.

3.

4.

5

Thoughts and Reflections
1. Are you looking forward to going home? Why or why not?

2. What will you miss most about your time on this mission trip?

3. Share with the group: What were one or two of the most amazing things you saw or experienced on this mission trip?

Take a moment to reveal your prayer partners for the week and share some things about how awesome they were during this mission trip.

Leader's Notes
There are several ways this reveal could be done creatively, depending on group size and the time allotted. The reveal can be thoughtfully combined with a foot-washing ceremony, so that each person reveals who they prayed for by washing that person's feet. Then that person will go wash the feet of the one they prayed for, and so on, one at a time, until everyone has revealed who they prayed for. This is just one idea. Going around in a circle and saying an encouraging word about your prayer partner and revealing who each person prayed for is also simple and profound.

 AWARE

1. What are some worries you have as you go back home?

2. What do you dread to facing?

3. What are you going to tell people when they ask how the mission trip was?

 DARE

1. Read Luke 10:1-2 and 17-20. We read on the first day when we arrived about the disciples being sent out two by two. In verses 17-20, it seemed as if the disciples had an amazing mission trip and as they are returning back from it, they are

in celebration mode. In what ways do you feel like them, and why?

2. What is the encouragement that Jesus gives to the them about their joy and celebration? Why do you think he gave such an encouragement (or warning)?

3. How can this inform you as you return back home?

 **PREPARE**

Evening Reflections

Morning Reflections

Reminders for the Team

Leader's Notes
Your teens and leaders will need to begin packing. Remind them of packing away dirty laundry in separate bags, being sure everything is dry, etc. Prepare them for return travels by talking about issues and procedures for traveling again. In chapters five and six, we discussed issues such as rest stops, van rides, and airport protocol.

We even discussed small things like bathroom break warnings, head counts, and bringing electronics. In these latter meetings, so it may stay fresh with the teens, it is important to reinforce these ideas again.

It will also be important to remind your team of the follow-up mission meetings you will have and the importance of them. The "mission" isn't over.

PRAYER

- Pray that our salvation in Christ may be the most celebrated aspect of the mission trip.

- Pray for those you have met who will be remaining behind when you leave.

- Pray for safe travels back home.

Dear Jesus...

ACT III | Meetings 13-15

13: MISSIONS BEGINS AT HOME

Personal Reading

Let's be real. It's different back at home. And perhaps in many good ways. You may appreciate having your own bathroom and bed even more now than before the trip. You may be thankful for the food in your refrigerator. You might be thankful to have free use of your phone or iPad. You can go online anytime. It is so much more convenient at home.

However, maybe you miss your mission trip already. Maybe you miss the people you met, miss your team, and miss serving God actively each day. This is true for many people who go on mission trips. So, don't feel bad about it. But the question is, how can you approach and embrace these feelings?

Your short-term mission trip was only the beginning. You prepared before you left, served daily on the mission field, and have now returned. Hopefully, before and during the trip you began to sense the importance of missions, not only during your "short-term" mission trip time, but long after. Because it is what God's church and his people are all about. It is who you were made to be.

My thoughts, feelings, fears, and joys right now...

MEETING #13

 **SHARE**

Leader's Notes
Pray: *Always open with a word of prayer.*

Share: *You can ask teens about their last journal entries in their books.*

Thoughts and Reflections
1. How are you doing since you returned home from your trip? What have been some ups and downs?

2. What are some of the differences you have found since coming back home? Is there anything you have observed or felt that is not the same as before you went?

3. On the trip, you were asked about relationships with people back at home, especially some of the difficult ones you have. Have any of them improved since returning home?

 **AWARE**

Leader's Notes
What You Will Need: *You will need toothpicks and a bag of mini-marshmallows for each group of 3-4 teens. Each group will be using the material to construct a church. (Optional: You can use Legos for this activity as well.)*

Break up into groups of three or four people. Each team will get their own identical set of building supplies.

Your team will have five minutes to build a church, using only the supplies you've been given.

 **DARE**

1. Go around to the different structures. Take time to look at each one and decide which one is the best depiction of a church. State the reasons why. You cannot vote for your own structure.

2. We know the church is not actually made of these unique building materials, but what is your church "made" of? Describe the best aspects of your church. What do you love about your church? What do you love about your youth group?

3. Think about any churches you have visited in the past, perhaps while you were on a vacation or traveling. What do you recall from visiting other churches?

Leader's Notes
Perhaps you may have visited a church on your mission trip as well and you can discuss that now.

The point of this time is to reflect upon and notice how we describe the church in terms of locations, programs, activities, and people. We easily go back to thinking that the church is a weekly "gathering." But we are called to not just gather on Sundays or on the mission field. Instead, the true identity of the church is always and continually "gathering," as you'll discuss next.

4. What is the true identity of the church, as we recall from Matthew 12:30? As we think about churches, let's remember again the true identity of the church.

5. What does this remind us again about "short-term" missions? Where and when does the mission start and end?

Leader's Notes
Try to emphasize that mission starts at home. It did not end when your team left the mission field. In other words, the "gathering" mission of the church is continual.

 **PREPARE**

Leader's Notes
Give your team the 3-2-1 Takeoff evaluation to do for next time. You'll find it on page 199 here, and your team will find it on page 133 of their journals.

1. Before our next meeting, please take time to do the 3-2-1 Takeoff Evaluation on page 133.

2. Reflect also on ideas about how the youth group can be active missionaries year round and not just "short term" or over the summer.

 **PRAYER**

- Spend time praying for those the team met on this mission trip and for those still at your location, like local people, missionaries, mission organizations you worked with, or friends you made during the mission trip.

- Spend time praying for the youth group as you seek to be more active in mission work year around.

Dear Jesus...

14: 3-2-1 TAKEOFF TO NEXT TIME

Personal Reading

There is a famous quote attributed to different people and sources. It says something like "You don't know where you're going until you know where you've been." Perhaps this quote is a variation of something said by philosopher George Santayana: "Those who are unaware of history are destined to repeat it."

Your mission trip was a great experience. But you don't want to live just in the past. The past is also not something just to be repeated. After the last meeting, you were asked to do the 3-2-1 Takeoff Evaluation. The purpose of it was to help you reflect on "where you've been," so you can keep going and moving forward as a person and even as a youth group. Missions begins at home, and hopefully your short-term mission trip will be a foundation to help you "take off" like a rocket for the future.

My thoughts, feelings, fears, and joys right now...

MEETING #14

 **SHARE**

Leaders Notes
This meeting will focus on using the 3-2-1 Evaluation Tool as a reflection for the past mission trip, as well as future mission trips and service year round, for each person.

Pray: *Always open with a word of prayer.*

Thoughts and Reflections
1. Are you considering going on a mission trip next summer? Why or why not? If not next summer, how about another time in the future?

2. In what ways can you and your youth group do missions year around and for your whole lives and not just during "short-term" time periods? What reflections and thoughts do you have personally and for the youth group?

3. Are any of you considering full-time vocational, long-term missionary service?

 **AWARE**

Leader's Notes
This time will be devoted to reviewing the 3-2-1 Evaluation. Feel free to use the added explanations on page 200 for processing it now with your youth. Walk through each part together, asking those who feel

comfortable to share their answers with the group, so that everyone can benefit.

Spend some time considering the 3-2-1 Evaluation you did after the last meeting. Remember that thoughtfulness with this evaluation with be helpful not just to the youth group but also to you personally.

DARE

1. Read Hebrews 10:24-25. How does this verse speak to you and the team as you think about "missions" in the future?

2. Think of your 3-2-1 Evaluation as a countdown to a "lift off" of sorts. The mission trip starts now. And whether the youth group is planning on doing service work sometime this year, whether you are thinking of an STM trip again in the future, or whether you become a person who supports missions and missionaries as a "sender," always remember that missions is not just a "short-term" idea.

PREPARE

1. This week at home, watch the video for Matthew West's "Do Something" on YouTube and listen closely to the lyrics for next time.

Link: https://www.youtube.com/watch?v=b_RjndG0IX8

2. After listening to the song, consider some people who "did something" for you that has impacted your life—a Sunday school teacher, a neighbor, a family member, etc. Whose actions and care have changed your life for the better?

Be prepared to share about some of those people next time and maybe even thank them personally this week for what they did that changed you. You can write some thoughts below.

 **PRAYER**

- Pray for mission work and a mission mindset to be part of your whole life.

- Pray for opportunities to serve others individually and as a youth group.

Dear Jesus...

15: JOURNEYING TO OUR FINAL HOME

Personal Reading

You're about to have your last and final mission trip meeting for THIS mission trip. It's kind of sad. However, even if it is your last meeting, you will probably see your friends from your mission team at youth group or school, and the memory of your trip will always be with you. That's a good thing.

As you remember your mission trip fondly, also look forward to what God has in store for your future. You have a long life to live, and God has even greater plans and purposes for you. Ephesians 2:10 says, "For we are his workmanship, created in Christ Jesus for good works, which God prepared beforehand, that we should walk in them" (ESV).

Did you hear that? You are created for good works, which God has prepared already. You have so much more to do for God. As you consider this truth, know that your life ahead is a long journey, which will take you on a great adventure, from today until you get to your final home.

My thoughts, feelings, fears, and joys right now...

MEETING #15

 **SHARE**

Leader's Notes
Pray: *Always open with a word of prayer.*

Share: *As your team shares about their "final home," this session could get a little emotional. Just be sensitive to this. Also, some sensitive theological/personal situations could arise, especially as it relates to a theology of heaven and who we may or may not eventually see there.*

If your team have people close to them who were non-believers who've passed away, discussing those people will be a sensitive issue.

What You Will Need: *During the **Thoughts and Reflections** portion of the meeting, you'll want to show the video for Matthew West's "Save a Place for Me," or at least listen to it as a group. (Note: Yes, it's another Matthew West song. No, this was not intentional. It really just fits.) You can even print out the lyrics and pass those out as well.*

Link: https://www.youtube.com/watch?v=zbsBUf9VKyc

Thoughts and Reflections
1. Have you ever lost some near to you? Would you be willing to share a little about that experience?

2. Let's watch the video for Matthew West's song called "Save a Place for Me" and read/listen carefully to the lyrics as we

hear this song. What are some thoughts when you hear this song? Who comes to mind for you?

I wanna live my life just like you did
And make the most of my time just like you did
And I wanna make my home up in the sky
Just like you did, oh, but until I get there
Until I get there, just save a place for me

Matthew West

Matthew West, "Save a Place for Me,"
Something to Say (album), Sparrow, 2008

3. Did you meet people on your mission trip who are making the most of their time as well?

4. Your "homework" from the last meeting was to watch the video for Matthew West's "Do Something." Who were the people you thought of who have "done something" in your life? Are any of them the same people you think of who you'd like to "save a place" for you in heaven?

 **AWARE**

1. Read Revelation 7: 9-11. What does this picture of heaven say about the people who will be there?

2. Think about this quote from author and pastor John Piper:

"Missions is not the ultimate goal of the church.
Worship is. Missions exists because worship
doesn't. Worship is ultimate, not missions, because
God is ultimate, not man. When this age is over,
and the countless millions of the redeemed fall
on their faces before the throne of God, missions
will be no more. It is a temporary necessity. But
worship abides forever. Worship, therefore, is the

fuel and goal in missions. It's the goal of missions because in missions we simply aim to bring the nations into the white-hot enjoyment of God's glory. The goal of missions is the gladness of the peoples in the greatness of God."

John Piper

Let the Nations Be Glad!: The Supremacy of God in Missions
(Grand Rapids, MI: Baker, 1993)

3. What are your reflections as you read this quote and consider our final "home"?

4. From the quote and from Revelation 7, what do you think we will be doing in heaven? What does this passage specifically say about what we may be doing in heaven?

5. How does this passage also remind you of all the different people you met this past summer? And where might you meet them again? How is it hopeful?

 **DARE**

Read Revelation 20:1-4. Let's close this phase of our mission trip with these verses.

1. What is the picture of our final home?

2. What is so hopeful about our final home?

3. How does it give you hope today?

 **PREPARE**

Leader's Notes
While this is the last formal mission meeting, you can continue to encourage teens to think about ways for the youth group to be "missionaries" year round.

Make sure to emphasize to teens that there is likely to be a time of post-mission-trip blues and that they can always come see any adult leader about whatever they are feeling or going through.

Congratulations. This is final meeting for this mission trip. While this is the last formal mission meeting, you can continue to think about ways for you and the youth group to be "missionaries" year round.

Remember that some of you will struggle in the coming months after such a great trip. That is natural. Please know you can always come see any adult leader about your struggles.

PRAYER

Let's close with these verses as a benediction for each of you. This is your life calling, not just a "short-term" calling.

**"Therefore go and make disciples of all nations,
baptizing them in the name of
the Father and of the Son and of the Holy Spirit,
and teaching them to obey everything
I have commanded you.
And surely I am with you always,
to the very end of the age."**

Matthew 28:19-20

Leader's Notes
Ask your group to read the verses aloud together as a prayer and blessing for their lives. If time and resources allow, you might even print the verse on small cards they can place on a mirror at home or bedside table, computer, etc., where they can be reminded of this calling all the time.

Dear Jesus...